Dave Kahle | The Heart o

Publisl

The DaCo (
P.O. Box 523
Comstock Park, MI 49321

May, 2014

Copyright MMXIV by Dave Kahle. All rights reserved.

Second edition

Dave Kahle Management, LLC
P.O. Box 523
Comstock Park, MI 48321
May, 2018

Published by Dave Kahle Management, LLC P.O. Box 523; Comstock Park, MI 49321
1.616.451.9377

ISBN 9781980916857

CONTENTS

Introduction

This is the twelfth book I have written, and by far the most difficult to write. I continually questioned the idea that my life and the challenges that I faced trying to be a Christian sales person were of interest to others.

I found it excruciatingly difficult to write about myself. Of all the other things that I have written, they have always been about ideas, practices, strategies to help people do better. Granted, I have illustrated them with anecdotes from my own career. But those were illustrations, not the subject of the article or book. This book is different. It's very personal.

On the balancing scale on which I weighed the decision as to whether or not to write it, the personal nature of the subject weighed heavily on the side against it. On the other hand, I had a number of people express interest in the stories and the lessons that I have learned along the way. I've interacted with tens of thousands of sales people in my seminars and private training programs, and I have grown to understand that my experiences have been unique. And, I know of no other book that deals with the conflict between the world's notions of what sales success should look like, and my evolving understanding of what Christ would want in that career.

You can tell which side of the balance scale weighed more heavily, as you are reading this book.

In the end, I felt the potential to shed some light on the conflict outweighed my inherent shyness. This is one person's story and one person's struggle. In it, however, I hope to provide some encouragement and direction to the generations of Christian sales people who come along. We can all learn from those of who have gone before us. Here's the story of one.

One

This is going to be tricky

I was a twenty-something, and only a year or two into my life as a Christian. We were having lunch in a restaurant in Ann Arbor, Michigan, and I sat across from my prospective employer, in the final interview for what was to be my first full time professional selling situation. During the interview process, I had learned from the sales recruiter with whom I was working that the previous salesperson, the one I would be replacing if I got the job, had been fired for lying on his call reports. The company, I believed, had acted in a way that indicated that honesty and integrity were important to them.

That fit perfectly with my newfound Christian ethics, and I wanted to appeal to that value in them. So, I mentioned that I was a "born-again Christian," and could be counted on to be honest. The interview ended with no job offer. Later that week, the sales recruiter indicated that my comment had frightened my prospective employer. He had been prepared to offer me the job, and had changed his mind at the last minute.

What if I used my job to proselytize the customers? I wasn't being hired to be a missionary, providing my testimony to every customer, I was being hired to sell his products.

On the prodding of the recruiter, we went back and forth a few times, and I was able to convince the sales manager that I would not try to proselytize my customers nor loudly proclaim my Christianity, but would be directed internally by its values.

I got the job, and so was introduced to the conflicts of being a Christian salesperson. This, I thought - being a Christian salesperson - is going to be tricky.

Being a Christian salesperson is going to be tricky!

This was to be my first really professional sales position. But, I wasn't new to selling. As a college student, I found a summer job working for the Jewel Tea Company.

A national company headquartered in the Chicago area, they eventually morphed into the chain of Jewel grocery stores that have come to dominate the Chicago area.

At the time, they sold groceries and household items to housewives from little panel trucks. The housewife would sign up for the service, and the Jewel Tea route salesperson would show up every two weeks, deliver the order from the last time, and take an order for delivery the next time. The route salespeople were checked onto their routes, and ran them like independent businesses. There were thousands of routes around the country.

I was one of hundreds of college students hired around the country to operate the route while the salesperson was on vacation.

Each route had a storage area – typically a garage, lined with shelves. Once a week, the truck from headquarters would disgorge the week's orders, and the salesperson would spend an evening organizing them.

Then, each day, we would load up the orders for that day, plus some "impulse items" like bags of candy or cookies, and head out for that day's route.

At each stop, we'd fill an aluminum basket with the items to be delivered -- the displays and marketing pieces for that round of calls, and a few of the impulse items.

The sales call began with a delivery of the order, proceeded to showing the displays for things like back to school clothes, or cookware. Then, there was always a large card with the grocery specials on it, from which we'd try to garner an order. Finally, we'd suggest a couple of the impulse items, write everything up on an order pad for the next visit, collect the money, and be on our way to the next customer.

I loved it. Not only did it feel good to be in charge of my own day, but I enjoyed the interaction with the customers, and, for the first time, felt the "high" that comes when someone says, "Yes." The impact of my efforts was measurable, and could be added up in dollars of sales.

And, amazingly, I would consistently sell more in my two weeks on the route than the regular salesperson did. I was dumbfounded. How could that be? I just did what they told me to do. Didn't everybody do that?

This was to become the foundation for my conviction, which is central to my work as a sales educator and sales trainer: That there are best practices in the profession of sales, and to excel at the job, you need to do what the best do.

There are best practices in the profession of sales, and to excel at the job, you need to do what the best do.

That sounds so common sense so as, on first glace, to hardly even warrant saying. But, over the next four decades, I was to discover that the overwhelming majority of salespeople don't bother to study or implement the best practices of their profession.

In my position as a route salesperson, I took the time to fill the basket before each sales call, so I always had something to sell, and always had something to talk about. A simple thing – a thing my bosses told me to do – but it set me apart from the older and more experienced sales people who didn't bother.

I did so well in that summer job that the company said that anytime I wanted to work, over Christmas or Spring break, for example, they would find something for me to do. I took them up on it, and spent my Christmas and Easter breaks working vacant routes. The second summer, they checked me onto a vacant route, and in the short ten weeks that I was there, I brought it up to a level with the best performing routes in the area.

That earned me a small scholarship as the best summer employee within the district, and a trip to Barrington, Illinois with other summer winners for an overnight visit to the headquarters and a steak barbeque with the president of the company! At 19 years old, it didn't get much better than that.

I began to see the perks that come with excelling at sales: more influence with the company, prospering financially, and special perks reserved for only the best. I began to culture a taste for the profession of sales.

But I had greater financial needs than could be met by just a summer job. So, I found a job during the school year selling men's clothing in B.R. Bakers, an expensive men's clothing store.

It was a typical retail store in what was then the exclusive shopping area in Toledo, Ohio. The casual clothes and furnishings (shirts & ties) were displayed in the front of the store, and the big ticket items -- suits, sport coats and dress slacks -- in the back. The job paid an hourly wage, plus a commission. The older more experienced employees sold the big ticket items, and the younger, part time help was relegated to the front of the store.

But, staffing requirements didn't always work out that way, and I soon transitioned to selling the more expensive suits and sport coats. Once again, I found exceptional success. I probably averaged about 30 – 40 hours per week, and consistently outsold everyone in all the branches. My sales were only exceeded by a couple of the real pros who operated out of our well-established downtown headquarters.

I really was at a loss to explain my success. I learned from my boss, and picked up tips from the buyers and manufacturer representatives who would visit from time to time. Once again, it was a matter of doing what my bosses told me to do, and then enhancing those "best practices" with others I gained along the way. I couldn't understand why I was more successful than most others. It really wasn't that difficult.

I'd greet the customer and try to find something to comment on or compliment, so that I'd begin a conversation with the customer. The other salespeople were satisfied using the old standard, "Can I help you?"

When it was clear that the customer was looking for a suit, sport coat, or other expensive item, I'd walk them back to their size on the rack, select something I thought they might like, and ask them to put it on just to check the size. I'd let them look through the selection and often would make a suggestion or two. If things went well, we'd have 3 – 4 possibilities identified.

I'd hang them on a separate rack, and focus the customer's attention on choosing among them. Often enough, the customer would elect to buy one of those suits. It just seemed so simple.

Again, I tasted the special benefits that come with being good at sales. I made more money than almost everyone else. When Oleg Cassini, a world famous clothing designer, came to town, I was selected to join him and the company executives at a cocktail party. Since I was seen as an asset to the company, I could set my own hours, and had first crack at the prime times on the schedule.

I enjoyed the money, the perks, and the feeling of success that came with that job, and continued working there part-time after I graduated.

It was in this period of time that I became a Christian. I came from a strong Catholic family, and attended Catholic elementary and high schools. But, I was always a bit of free thinker, and had a dose of independent, maverick spirit, so I soon grew disenchanted with the rules, regulations and rigid hierarchy of that institution, and left it, mentally, in my teen years.

For the next few years, I think I passed through every mental landscape through which a seeker could journey: Zen, Buddhism, Agnosticism, Atheism, and strident humanism. But I saw faults with every one if these "isms", and felt a yearning inside – something missing – that none of these philosophies could fill. It was then that someone handed me *"The Late, Great Planet Earth,"* the famous book by Hal Lindsey.

His graphic descriptions of the last days shook me like nothing else in my life, and I soon found myself studying the Bible one-on-one with a minister. Shortly thereafter, I made a commitment to Christ, and, at age 22, was baptized.

A year or so later, still in the emotional and spiritual rush of my recent conversion, I found myself sitting across from my future manager at lunch in Ann Arbor.

Chapter Two

You Should Feel Conflicted!

If only our friends behind the pulpits, or those in more 'regular' jobs, had a clue as to the conflicts that we face, they may have, somewhere along the line, been able to provide some direction. Then, maybe, the job of the Christian salesperson wouldn't be so lonely.

It is a position that is characterized by conflicts. The business world holds certain values and strategies as unassailable paradigms, and teaches them with passion, sincerity and good intentions. Many of these conflict with our Christian values and paradigms. For example, the sales success industry tells you to strive to achieve, to accumulate more material things. On the other hand, our Christian values tell us it is more important to become than it is to achieve. To give is more blessed than to receive. Our lives are not measured by accumulation, but by the status of our relationship with Christ. That's a conflict.

The sales success industry preaches overcoming your weaknesses and building new skills. Yet the Christian community is enabled by the power of the Holy Spirit and the expression of His gifts, not the strengths of the individual. In-tune Christians exercise their gifts, and give their weaknesses to Christ. That's a conflict.

The business world emphasizes "doing it right." Sales books are full of the right words to say, the right techniques to use. The emphasis is often on the technique. A deeper Christian understanding proceeds from a realization that it is more important to do the right things. Techniques are less important than motivations, and the essence of a human's accomplishment is more accurately assessed by the direction of his heart.

This is hardly the end of the list. But you get the idea. As Christian salespeople, we feel like we're doing the splits, with one foot firmly caught in the world, and the other pulling us away, and deeply embedded by the church.

It's no wonder we feel conflicted.

But there's more. The ultimate conflict is that which comes from inside. I'm speaking here about the conflict with the teachings of the institutional church. There is a conflict which infuses everything that a Christian salesperson does. Almost every plan, every decision, every action, is made within the context of this enormous, career long conflict.

On one hand, we are taught that we are not responsible for the outcomes, that God controls the end result – that our job is to stay in tune to God's leading, adhere to His principles, and stick to His ordinances, and let Him, then, determine the outcomes.

This is a fundamental message of the Christian church. It's a mantra that is taught repetitively from the pulpit, in Sunday schools, in small groups, in Christian publications, and everywhere the church reaches.

Because it is such a deeply imbedded paradigm, we see it popping up in all kinds of places. It is how we explain a missionary who has labored for ten years in a mission field with no results. Or a church that is generations old but has not grown for decades. It is what allows us to make a place for the church secretary with no computer skills – "After all," we think, "she's a good person and needs a job."

On the other hand, we live and work in a world that demands performance. I cannot imagine a circumstance where a salesperson who sold nothing for a few years would be allowed to keep his job. A business that never grew would soon be out of business. And an unqualified, unskilled employee would likely not even be in contention for the job – regardless of how good a person he or she was.

The sales profession, perhaps more than any other, is driven by results and performance. Our actions result in measurable results, and our employers continually manage and monitor those results. Often, our income and our jobs depend on us achieving acceptable results.

So, on one hand we have the proclamations of the church that we are not responsible for results. On the other, we have the demands of the job that say, "Oh yes you are." That conflict is at the heart of the Christian salesperson's psyche.

Which leads us to this question: "Can we successfully navigate the turbulent waters that exist between these two seemingly conflicting world views and sets of paradigms? " Can we be a Christian sales person?

I think the answer is YES. And I'm going to share with you how I came to that position.

Chapter Three

My first professional sales position

Since I had foresworn my desire to proselytize my customers, my manager decided that I was a risk worth taking, and hired me to work the state of Michigan for H. C. Electronics.

The primary product the company sold was a system of amplification equipment for classrooms called Phone Ear®. It was highly technical, and required that the salesperson have an understanding of the ultimate user – the hearing impaired elementary student, and the details of the equipment.

Off I went for six weeks of training in Mill Valley, California, just across the Golden Gate Bridge from San Francisco – my first official, professional sales training. We spent time learning the intricacies of the company, as well as the technical nature of the product. Most of our time, however, was spent in highly structured sales training classes. There were about a half dozen of us, and sales training consisted of memorizing two single spaced, multiple-page documents that comprised the two presentations that we were required to give. We would role-play the presentation in front of the assembled class and various company executives, have it video-taped, and then critique it together. The next day, we'd do it again, and were expected to be better at it.

I remember my sales manager, in an effort to show up the other managers who sent new salespeople to the training program, pressured me to memorize the first presentation prior to the training, and then encouraged me to be the first volunteer.

And so I did. (There I was again; just doing what my boss told me to do.) I did a passable job as the first role-play volunteer and was relieved to have the first one behind me. I was eager to see how my performance compared to the other trainees.

EEEK! None of them were at all prepared. They hadn't even begun to work on the scripts. I looked like a shining star, and my sales manager looked like a genius. (There was a little lesson learned. Do well, and do what your boss tells you to do, and you make him look good. And that's always good for you!)

A little lesson learned: Do what your boss tells you, and do it well, and you make him look good. And that's always good for you!

After six weeks of training, I returned home to start my new career as a professional salesperson. Off I went to visit my existing customers and to open up contact with future prospects.

Oops! Things weren't quite like I was led to believe. It turned out that my predecessor hadn't been all that reliable. I encountered customer after customer who was upset at the lack of response from the previous salesperson. Evidently, his tenure was characterized by broken promises, unreturned phone calls, and generally lousy service.

They were waiting for me with both barrels loaded, and I got blasted almost everywhere I'd been.

It shook me up. Here I thought I had such a great product – state of the art, advanced electronics – it could do wonders for the kids who got it. And yet, I couldn't even talk about it because my customers were more intent on complaining about the previous sales person. That animosity was automatically transferred to me, as the representative of the company.

I couldn't give my meticulously prepared, memorized and practiced two -page presentation if no one would listen to me. So, I decided to apologize for the previous guy and point out that I was not him. I determined to return every phone call as quickly as possible, to follow up on every communication, and to be as reliable as I could be.

It was a revelation to me. No matter how good the product, or how solid the company, if they don't like you, they are not going to be receptive to your message.

A little lesson learned: No matter how good the product, nor how solid the company, if they don't like you, they are not going to be receptive to your message.

It took a while, but gradually I was able to develop my own reputation, and the animosity gradually faded away.

My first sale was made to a rural special education system, off the beaten track, that I happened upon. They had never heard of the system and were awed by its features. Better yet, they had no experience with the previous salesperson.

The most embarrassing event of my sales career happened half-way through my tenure as a Phone Ear salesperson. I was growing more sure of myself. I had a number of successes under my belt, was growing to be respected by my customers, and had come to understand the real advantages my product had relative to the competition.

The City of Detroit had a big opportunity. Ten classrooms of equipment, the largest single opportunity of my tenure. All the other competitors were represented, including the Detroit area distributor that represented my arch competitor. I worked through the bureaucratic obstacle course that was their purchasing system until I finally got an audience with the head of the program, who would have the final say.

Earlier that year, one of my customers had shown me the competitor's product, and pointed out that the salesperson had shared a slight problem with the batteries working loose, and that they had solved the problem by wrapping a rubber band around the battery pack.

When I demonstrated the equipment to the department head, I pointed out our battery pack, and casually mentioned that the competition held theirs together with rubber bands.

That comment struck a raw nerve with her. She stopped my presentation, and said, "Do you know what I don't like about you? You are so negative about the competition."

I was stunned. My face turned beet red, I started to sweat and had no comment. I'm not sure how that sales call ended, other than very shortly thereafter. Her comment upset me for a week.

The deal, of course, went to the competition.

Not only was the sales call excruciatingly embarrassing, but I was further embarrassed by not getting the deal. Another little lesson learned: Never speak badly about the competition.

Another little lesson learned:
Never speak badly about the competition.

By this time, I was becoming accustomed to success. I was intent on doing a good job and becoming successful. Every night, before a presentation, I would check all the demo equipment, rehearse my presentation, and review all the possible questions and answers.

In the 30 or so months that I sold Phonic Ear, there were 29 major purchases in my territory. I got 28. Detroit was the one that got away.

But I was a young and naive salesperson, and had a lot to learn. That's specifically what one of the competitive salespeople (the rubber band guy) said to me at a trade fair.

The profession got together for an annual meeting and trade fair, and I, and all my competitors, were there, displaying our wares. There were a couple dozen booths, arranged in a large hall. My rubber band competitor had the booth next to me. At this point, I had some rapport with the customers, as did my competitor. We eventually developed an easy and casual banter among us.

My company had just introduced a revolutionary product – a portable device that was designed to test the distortion levels of a hearing aid. Prior to this, testing distortion was something that happened in acoustic laboratories with expensive equipment and trained technicians. Now, audiologists and teachers of the hearing impaired could test the acoustics of every kid's hearing aid.

It was the hit of the show. I tested all our equipment for our customers, as well as the hearing aids that they brought. My competitor, in the next booth over, took a break. When he was gone, we lifted his product from the display, tested it, and put it back. Of course, it showed distortion levels far greater than mine.

When he came back, one of our customers confronted him with that. When he discovered what we had done, he looked at me and said, "You've got a lot to learn about competition." Another embarrassment. He was right, of course. I did have a lot to learn. I was sneaky and out of line.

Looking back from this perspective, I'd have to say that I didn't see God as being much involved with me in this job. I was so intent on learning the job and doing well that I didn't give much thought to God's role in that. In fact, He, or more accurately my perception of Him, almost prevented me from getting the job.

As a young Christian, I pretty much believed everything coming out of the pulpit and Bible school classes. I accepted the common paradigm: Church was what you did on Sundays. There were two worlds: The sacred, which was the church and every program and meeting that it sponsored, and the secular, which was my job, among other things. The two didn't meet. If I wanted to attain to any kind of spirituality, I'd have to be more involved with the church. My job got in the way of that, as it prevented me from attending the mid-week meetings. Because I was a full-time salesperson, I was a second-class Christian.

Or, so I believed at the time.

Because I was a full-time salesperson, I was a second-class Christian. Or, so I believed at the time.

Chapter Four

Big Lessons Learned: Be good at your job.

I've learned some big lessons – lessons that apply to almost every aspect of our jobs. And, in some cases, to our lives.

Many of these big lessons came as I reflected on my experience and assembled observations and conclusions that directly contradicted some of the paradigms that had been instilled in me.

One of these, perhaps the biggest, I've already mentioned in Chapter Two: The conflict between "being a good person" and "producing good results." The church teaches "be a good person," while the world demands, "produce good results."

There are some significant benefits that accrue to the Christian salesperson who excels at his/her job. In every profession, those who excel at that profession are naturally and universally ceded more respect than the mass of that profession. This is especially true in sales. The best salespeople are looked on as a bit wiser, smarter, and more dedicated than the others.

Not only do their peers hold them up for greater respect, but so does the company's management. They lend their ears to the opinions and ideas of the best salespeople and weigh those opinions more heavily than those of the average salespeople.

21

In my first sales position, as a college student working a summer job, I was sent to the company's headquarters in Barrington, Illinois and spent some time chatting with the president of the company. Why? Because I was the region's top salesperson.

In my retail career, I was asked to come downtown and meet with the company's president. Why? Because I was the store's top salesperson.

I can continue with these examples, but you get the idea. Success in sales affords you respect and influence with both your peers as well as your employers. And that is something for which I believe every Christian salesperson should strive. If we are going to be a light to the world, we ought to be the brightest light that we can be, illuminating the greatest amount of darkness possible.

**If we are going to be a light to the world,
we ought to be the brightest light that we can be,
illuminating the greatest amount of darkness possible.**

From a practical point of view, success in sales, i.e. being good at our jobs and rising above the ranks of our colleagues, is, I believe, one of the first principles of a Christian salesperson.

But we still haven't resolved the conflict between the conflicting paradigms: "It's all in God's hands, just let it happen," and "I want to be the best."

Here's how we can navigate the tricky waters between these seemingly opposing paradigms.

We don't make the decision to buy. Our customers do that, usually on their own, and often when we are not there. Our results are the measurement of the transactions created by our customer's decisions. So, ultimately, we don't control the results. The results are, in the end, up to our customers, at times influenced and directed by God.

But we do control our actions. And our actions influence the customer's decisions. The greater the quantity and quality of our actions, the more likely it is that we will influence the customer's decisions, and we'll impact the results.

I like to think of it as process and results. We don't dictate the results. But we do influence them by focusing on the process that precedes the customer's decision.

Let me illustrate from a couple of my sales positions. When I was running vacation routes for the Jewel Tea Company, I would often outsell the permanent, much more experienced salesperson whose place I was filling while he/she was on vacation.

How could that be? Here I was, the inexperienced young college student. What did I know about selling?

I was taught to make sure the basket was full of impulse items for every sales call, and to point out one or two things on the "specials" card. I would just point to a couple of things, and say something like, "This is a really good buy." Or "A lot of people like these." While the customer was looking through the specials, I would flip back through the older invoices, and find a couple of things she had purchased in the past and ask if she needed more of them. That was it. Just doing a few things, with discipline, that my bosses taught me to do.

In a more fundamental sense, I attended to the process. As a result of doing the right things, and doing enough of them, more people made decisions to buy. I was amazed by how simple it was.

In my days of selling men's clothing in the retail store, I found the same things to be true. There were steps to the process. If someone came in looking for a suit or sport coat, I'd get him to try on something. From there, I'd try to have him select two or three options, and then help him narrow it down. When he got down to one or two, I'd encourage him to step into the dressing room and try on the pants. Most people would decide to take the suit when they saw how both pieces looked. After I had fit the suit, when the customer was back in the dressing room, I'd carry the suit jacket to the front of the store and slide a dress shirt into it and select a couple of ties to go with it. When he came out of the dressing room, I'd motion for him to come up and look at the shirt and ties. Frequently, we'd add those to the total sale.

Once again, it was a matter of me doing enough of the right things, in the right ways, to influence the results. I didn't make the decision. The customer did. But I attended to the process, focusing on doing the right things in the right way.

One more example from the world of institutional sales. When I sold amplification equipment to classrooms of hearing impaired children, it was important that I demonstrate the equipment to the people making the decision. The night before every demonstration, I would clean up the equipment, test it to make sure everything was as it should be, and then practice the demonstration. As a result, I made effective demonstrations, and was awarded 28 of the 29 major purchases in my territory.

I didn't make the decision. The customers did. The results were in their hands, not mine. But I did the right things, in the right way, and so influenced the customer. I attended to the process, not the results.

I did the right things, in the right way, and so influenced the customer.

I attended to the process, not the results.

That, then, is the key for a Christian salesperson. Leave the results up to Lord and your customers. Focus, instead, on the process. Do enough of the right things; do them in the right ways.

Be guided by Colossians 3:23:

23 Whatever you do, work at it with all your heart, as working for the Lord, not for men, 24 since you know that you will receive an inheritance from the Lord as a reward. It is the Lord Christ you are serving.

And don't forget Ecclesiastes:

Whatever your hands find to do, do it with all your might, for in the grave, where you are going, there is neither working nor planning nor knowledge nor wisdom. Ecclesiastes 9:10

Christian sales people ought to be the best. The top of the pile, the head of the pack. They ought to be so sought after that every manager ought to celebrate when he hires one, and every company pleased to have one.

Strive to be good at your job. It's the first principle for a Christian salesperson.

Chapter Five

God sees me through and teaches me a big lesson

A couple of years at H. C. Electronics, Inc. and I found myself on the top of the pack. I was the company's top sales person. I had a nice salary, a motivating bonus, a company car and a job that was becoming progressively easier. So, I became bored.

I didn't see any long-term opportunities with the company. The next step up the ladder was to become a regional manager, and all of those positions were firmly held by relatively young and able people. And, while I was comfortable, I was itchy for another challenge.

I registered with a head-hunter (the same one who had helped me find the job with H.C. Electronics, Inc.), and started to look at other opportunities.

Along came U.S. Surgical. What an interesting company. They had a product – surgical staplers -- that did all kinds of wonderful things for the surgeons and their patients. But the product was relatively new, and they were fighting the "20 year rule of thumb" in the surgical industry. That rule states that from the time a product or technique is proven to be more effective, it takes 20 years for it to be routinely accepted and used.

To help a surgical team become more comfortable with the product, the sales people were trained to actually scrub in surgery. You've seen it on TV. A surgeon stands at a special "scrub sink" and methodically scrubs every part of his hands a prescribed number of times, in a prescribed method, prior to putting on the gloves and gown and entering the sterile area of the surgical room. That's what we did. Right there with the surgeons and scrub nurses. We were gloved and gowned and had access to the inner most area of the surgery. Talk about heady stuff! Sales people actually did that.

Of course, we were thoroughly trained. But here was the catch. The position was the opposite of my previous one in a number of ways. It paid straight commission, for example, with a draw that lasted only the first six months. The salespeople bought their own demonstration samples and literature from the company.

I was enticed by the challenge. Before I accepted the offer, I calculated the amount of existing business in the territory. I felt that, if I could double the business within the first year, I'd be OK. After that, any increases would be real increases in my standard of living.

So I took the plunge and went off to New York for six weeks of intense training. While I was gone, the district sales managers changed, and I had a new boss. When I returned home from training, I was quickly met by my new district sales manager, who announced that he had rearranged the territories. The territory for which I was hired wasn't exactly the territory I was actually going to receive. In fact, the territory I ended up with had only about 30 percent of the existing business on which I was depending. My livelihood and the health and wellbeing of my family was in serious jeopardy.

I was outraged. How could they do this to me? What kind of a company was this that would treat its employees that way? I immediately decided that I didn't want to work for them and began looking for a different job. However, it only took a few weeks of interviewing for me to realize that I was unemployable. Most people with whom I interviewed viewed my quick desire to leave as a weakness in me, not a flaw in the company.

One thing led to another and, after six months, I owed the company $10,000 (a lot of money then), my draw was finished, and I had few prospects for finding another job. I found myself between a rock and a hard place!

I grew bitter and angry about my situation. How could they do this to me? My attitude influenced my behavior, and I found it almost impossible to sell the product. My bitterness grew and morphed into depression. There was no hope.

Then I had a realization. I finally saw, in a moment of blinding clarity, that my situation was pretty much my own doing. It wasn't them, it was *me*!

Yes, they had done a nasty deed to me. Yes, I had been dealt with unfairly. However, it was still a great product, and the opportunity was still substantial. The reason I wasn't selling anything was me! It was my bitterness, my depression, and my negative attitude that was influencing my behavior and thus my results.

Lesson Learned: The cause of my poor attitude, and the resulting poor performance was me!

The realization of my personal responsibility was like a great weight off my shoulders. If the problem was me, I could do something about it! I was once again in a situation where I could influence the world around me and impact my life. I was no longer a victim, depressed under the unjust weight of someone else's actions.

Since the problem was me, the power to do something was also in me! I saw the problem as having two dimensions: First, at the level of my job and my day-to-day activities, I needed to change my attitude and become more positive.

But there was also a deeper dimension. I was a Christian, convinced of the power of God to work in my life. Yet I sure wasn't living that conviction out. If I really thought that "all things work together for good for those that love the Lord," (Romans 8:28) then my attitude and behavior was not reflecting that. I needed an adjustment in my spiritual life and have that spill over into my attitude.

So, I decided to attack the problem (me) on both levels. If I could do away with my bitterness and negativity, I could be more effective. I needed to stop thinking so negatively and to change my attitude. From the spiritual point of view, if I could strengthen my relationship with God, and somehow channel some of His power into my attitude and my job, I could impact my thoughts, my attitude, and my results.

30

I reasoned that I needed to put positive, confident thoughts into my head. If I could fill my head with positive thoughts, I'd gradually be able to change my negative attitude.

At the time, I was living on the outskirts of my territory, and I had a daily 45-minute drive into the metropolitan Detroit area on Interstate 96. I decided to make use of that 45 minutes every morning to put positive thoughts into my head.

I spent a week finding powerful, positive promises in the Bible, as well as some other sources, and wrote them on "3 X 5" cards. Then, each morning, I'd hold the deck of "3 X 5" cards in front of me on the steering wheel, and flip through them over and over -- reading them repetitively as I drove into the city. One such quote, for example, was this:

"If God is with you, who can be against you?"

Over the next few months, I found myself growing spiritually. I became to expect God to work in my life and my job. My bitterness and resentment melted away, and I became calmer and more confident. As I bathed my mind in positive, confident ideas, I discovered my attitude gradually changing.

In six months I was able to pay off the debt, and I began making more money than I had imagined possible. What was an absolutely hopeless and miserable situation changed into one of the most financially rewarding, satisfying experiences of my life. Not only was I out of the miserable situation I had been in, but I discovered a level of peace of mind and spiritual awareness that I had not previously known.

The change in my circumstances occurred when I realized I was responsible for my situation, and that my negative attitude was impacting my life. I took action to consistently feed my mind positive and uplifting thoughts, and to tap into the power of God. Over a short time, I saw my attitude change. My attitude changed my behavior, and my changed behavior produced much better results.

It was really change from the inside out.

Big Lesson Learned: You can control your attitude!

Chapter Six

Big Lesson Learned: Personal responsibility

Imagine. An adult, mid-twenties, who just figured it out that his success was his responsibility! That was me. Looking back on it, it seems so blatantly obvious. Doesn't everyone know that? Unfortunately, the answer is NO. In fact, many people never get it. They never gain a deep and abiding belief that one is responsible for one's own behavior as well as the consequences of that behavior.

That seems so basic and common sense, yet I am constantly amazed by how few people actually exhibit it. Over and over in my work in developing sales people and their managers, I'm struck by how many people fail to accept responsibility for their own success or lack of it.

It's far more popular to be a victim. We have all shook our heads sadly over some newspaper account of someone who commits some act of irresponsibility, and then successfully sues someone else. In our litigious world, being a victim often pays. That is an unfortunate consequence of an unhealthy belief.

As long as we view ourselves as victims, we're unable to change ourselves or our circumstances and achieve better results. It is not our fault that we're not doing better, we tell ourselves. Someone else caused it. And because it's someone else's doing, the power to fix it and make it better is with someone else. We're powerless to fix it.

While few people admit it, or even realize it consciously, this "victim attitude," the direct opposite of personal responsibility, is very common, and embraced to some degree by most of us. This is especially true of sales people, who could always do better if only something were different – something that someone else controls. If only...*we had lower prices....our quality was better...the boss was more understanding ...customer service was more responsive...*you know the litany because you've chanted it.

My wife is a crises counselor. One of the biggest eye-openers for her occurred when she realized that she was counseling the same people over and over again. You'd think, as she did, that a crisis would be an isolated event. Not so. Many of her clients find themselves lurching from one crisis to another. Why? Because they don't make the changes in their behavior and character that got them into the crises in the first place. At some deep level, they see themselves as victims, not personally responsible for their own character, their own behavior, and the consequences that behavior brings. Where there is no sense of personal responsibility, there is little hope for positive change.

My results began to change also. Things began to go better. Six months later, I had paid off the debt to the company, and was making more money than I thought possible. The job became more fun, more financially rewarding and more fulfilling than anything I ever expected.

The turning point for me occurred at the moment I accepted personal responsibility for my circumstances.

Once again, the lesson is clear: When there is no acceptance of personal responsibility, there is little hope for positive change. Where there is personal responsibility, the future holds unlimited potential.

When there is no acceptance of personal responsibility, there is little hope for positive change.

Where there is personal responsibility, the future holds unlimited potential.

If you are committed to being best that you can be, then you must accept the idea that it is your personal responsibility to make the changes in behavior that will improve your results.

Chapter Seven

US Surgical

Imagine a selling situation where you (the salesperson) actually go into surgery and stand at the incision with the surgeon -- gloved, gowned and in the midst of the innermost circle. That was the signature sales strategy of US Surgical.

You can imagine the intense training that sales people had to go through. Six weeks in mid-town Manhattan, which is where the company's offices were at that point. Every morning, upon arrival at the offices, we were given a quiz on the previous day's material. Any one scoring less than 80 percent was fired and sent home.

After the intellectual content was mastered, we spent most of the training day at a dog lab in the South Bronx, practicing our skills with the surgical staplers on anesthetized dogs.

This was intense, heady stuff.

It was a long-term, complex selling cycle. Typically, it began in the hospital purchasing office with an introductory call to the appropriate purchasing agent to try to get his/her blessing and the name of the Operating Room Supervisor.

The next step was to try to get an appointment with the ORS (operating room supervisor). These were typically very busy, middle-aged nurses, who were among the strongest, toughest ladies in the hospital. In addition to being responsible for the most intense high-tech area of the hospital, they were used to telling the surgeons what to do, and in the hospital pecking order, the surgeons were at the top of the list. The ORSs didn't have a lot of time for sales people.

The ORS was the keystone of the sales process. She had to approve my presence in her operating room suite and could go a long way to facilitating my success or standing in the way of it.

If I couldn't get an appointment with the ORS, I'd try to see one of the surgeons, either in the hospital or at his office, interest him in the staplers, and then ride his coat tails into the OR and an appointment with the ORS.

The good graces of the ORS was so important to the sale, that I'd go to any lengths to nurture it. The story was told (it may be apocryphal) about one US Surgical sales person who was repeatedly denied an audience with the ORS of a large hospital. Out of frustration, he waited in the employee's parking lot, and noted which car she drove home. The next day, during her working shift, he let the air out of one of her tires. At the end of her shift, as she was preparing to drive home and was confronted with the flat tire, he showed up, and fixed the tire for her. The next time he called, she couldn't refuse the appointment.

I'm not sure that's a true story….

Regardless, I'd try to get the ORS to allow me to display and demonstrate the staplers to the surgeons for a day or two, or maybe a full week.

At that point, I'd show up at 6:30 AM at the hospital with a box of donuts. I'd change into surgical greens so that I looked like a surgeon (not a sales person) and set up my wares in the surgeon's lounge, or some other convenient spot.

It was here that I added a little wrinkle that seemed to make a difference. In a sea of light blue and light green colors, where there was always a lot of commotion and activity in the environment, I found it difficult to catch the surgeon's attention and focus them on the instruments. So, I bought a yard of burnt orange velvet. I kept it in my brief case, and would lay it down on top of the gurney or where ever I had space. I would arrange the staplers on top of that.

The burnt orange stood out in the OR suite, attracting everyone's attention. The stainless steel instruments, all polished and shiny, looked like jewelry against the velvet back ground. It caught their eye.

When the surgeons wandered by before their cases, I would demonstrate the staplers to them, doing everything I could to get them involved with the staplers. If they showed some interest, I'd all use the same close that we were trained to use: "Doctor, if you'd like to try this instrument, I'd be happy to scrub your next case with you."

With an affirmative response, I'd shortly find myself in surgery, standing across from the surgeon, instructing the nurses in how to handle the instruments, and doing the same for the surgeon. It wasn't until the surgeon pulled the handle and actually used the stapler that I made any money.

But using it one time didn't bring the surgeon to competence with the instruments, and I'd typically scrub four to eight cases with a surgeon before he felt comfortable enough with the instruments to go it alone.

I'd have maybe a half dozen surgeons in the process of learning to use the instruments. So, I'd call the surgical suite toward the end of the day, find out who was doing what surgeries and when, and then line up the day to go from one surgery to another. Occasionally, a surgeon would call and would want me for a specific case. I wore a beeper (this was pre-cell phone days). It was not uncommon to hear a message like this: "Hey Dave, I have a gun-shot wound. Can you come in and scrub it with me?"

After a while, I become a respected, regular member of the surgical team, and was invited to the holiday parties and after-hours get togethers.

In practice, it wasn't anything near smooth and uneventful. Surgery is an intense, highly technical process, with lots of variables. For instance, if the patient is running a fever, the doctor will postpone the case, not wanting to deal with the implications of an existing infection. It wasn't unusual, then, for a case to be postponed in the morning of the day it was scheduled. That could be frustrating.

I had a surgeon eager to use the staplers in a small rural hospital about 90 minutes' drive from my house. These major cases were typically scheduled for the first thing in the morning – 7 AM. We'd want to be in the hospital, in greens, at least a half hour before the case, which mean 6:30 AM.

Subtract 90 minutes' drive time from that, and you have me leaving the house at 5 AM, and getting out of bed at 4:30 AM. Four days in a row, as I walked into the surgical suite with my box of donuts under one arm, and the briefcase that held the staplers in another, the ORS, greeted me with, "Oh. Didn't anyone call you? The case has been postponed. The patient is running a temperature. " I turned around and went home.

You can imagine what kind of learning experience it was. Not only did I become competent and confident with all the procedures and policies of various surgical suites and surgeries, but I created relationships with most of the prominent surgeons in the northern suburbs of Detroit.

The experience punctured one of my illusions – that surgeons (or doctors in general) were refined, educated people of moderate temperaments. The language in the locker rooms was just as course and crude as a truck stop, and the jokes often just as vulgar.

One incident in particular stands out in my memory. I was working with an inner city hospital in Detroit, which was the preferred practice site for an oncology surgeon. He was a former star collegiate football player and looked the part – maybe 6'4", 240 pounds, gruff and intimidating.

Early in his experience with the staplers, he had a particularly challenging case – multiple tumors in the lower intestines. It was a difficult and long case. After about four hours, he came to the part of the procedure where he could use the staplers. The particular stapler that was appropriate for the procedure needed four centimeters of viable tissue in order to function effectively. Less than that, and the stapler was not to be used.

Rarely could you use a ruler to measure, so that, in some cases, it was a judgment call. In this particular case, the tissue was deep in the body cavity, and barely visible. You couldn't see it well enough to make a decision, so you had to estimate it by feel, and then make the decision.

The surgeon didn't want to make the call. He asked me to tell him. "Feel down there, "he said, "and tell me whether we have enough tissue to use it."

I had no business taking on that decision. "You need four centimeters of tissue" I said. "It is your decision." We went back and forth several times, with the surgeon becoming more insistent that I make a recommendation. I refused.

Finally, he decided to go ahead and use the stapler.

It didn't go well. Remember, we are now five hours into an extremely difficult surgery, the stress is at unbelievable levels, and the surgeon just encountered a major problem of his own doing. He blew up. "You S.O.B." he screamed, 'You killed my patient!" I screamed back. "I had nothing to do with it. It was your choice."

We went back and forth, screaming at each other, for maybe two or three minutes, he on one side of the patient, pacing back and forth, me on the other. He calmed down, and went back to work, completing the surgery over the next two or three hours, and treating me civilly. Afterward, in the surgeon's lounge, we both apologized. I, however, was upset for days.

There is an interesting postscript to this story. I called the hospital later in the week to inquire about the status of the patient -- recovering normally and doing well. What an amazing testimony to the recuperative power of our bodies!

That particular surgeon became an advocate of the staplers and used them whenever he could. The hospital had no capital budget and had no money to purchase the staplers, although the staples were billed to the patient, as are all the items used in the surgery. So, on the basis of that particular surgeon's busy schedule, I bought a set of staplers and donated them to the hospital. It cost me $3,000. However, I made that back in three months on the commissions I received from the staples used by that one surgeon.

One of the big lessons learned had to do with investing in future growth.

Remember, we were all on 100% commission, and paid our own expenses.

I discovered the wisdom of making investments in the growth of my business.

The case above was one such investment.

Lesson Learned: There are times and places to make an investment in your future growth.

Occasionally, I'd run into a surgeon who wanted to practice using the staplers before using them on a live patient. I made arrangements with a local dog lab. They would anesthetize a stray dog from the local animal shelter, and I'd meet the surgeon for a lesson and practice session. Just as in training, the dogs were then euthanized. The dog lab cost me about $100 per session, with absolutely no guarantee that the surgeon would use the staplers as a result.

But the biggest investment occurred when I decided to organize seminars.

It worked like this: I'd get some well-known surgeon who was a stapler advocate to agree to speak at a luncheon meeting. Then, I'd offer a free seminar to prospective surgeons. Come to a free lunch, hear this guy speak, and then go spend the afternoon in the dog lab. We'd arrange for lunch in a private room at a good local restaurant, promote the seminar, and I'd pick up the whole tab. These were small groups – maybe 4 – 8 surgeons at a time. But each seminar cost well over $1,000. Again, this expense was a speculative investment in my future.

An interesting aside: The restaurant I used most often was Machus Red Fox, the same restaurant from which Jimmy Hoffa disappeared.

Those seminars were one of the things that stimulated my business. They were a way to train multiple surgeons at one time, multiplying my efforts. I did them as often as I could.

Lesson Learned:
I could multiply my effectiveness by giving seminars.

The business grew. As one surgeon became adept at using the staplers, I'd continue to receive income from the staples used, and move on to another one. Eventually, I was making more money than I had ever imagined.

Being involved in surgery is a powerful experience, and in a long case, you often felt like you bonded with the other members of the surgical team. I felt some affinity for one – a male scrub nurse. We became friends, and, at some point, I shared my testimony to him. That resulted in a series of bible studies with he and his wife, and that resulted in both of them coming to Christ. It was the first time, as far as I know, that living my faith impacted a business acquaintance so positively for the Lord.

While it lasted, it was a great job. Not only was I making an excellent income, I had no real supervision and could work whatever hours I chose. I had created a reputation as a knowledgeable professional and was welcomed in almost every surgical suite in my territory.

But, this good thing was coming to an end. While the product was great, the money fantastic, and the sales situation fulfilling, the company's management was, at least from our perspective, erratic.

In the three years that I sold for US Surgical, I had four regional sales managers, each one lasting six to eight months. Various dictates

45

would come down from the corporate office, and a few months later, they would be contradicted. The corporate office handed down edicts with a heavy hand. Every quota was mandatory and accompanied by the threat of losing your job if you didn't perform.

I tried to stay under the radar of corporate scrutiny and hoped that my stellar sales performance would buffer me from the harsher mandates.

The company introduced a new staple for use in one of its instruments. In typical top-down fashion, every sales person was given a mandatory quota: "Sell X of these by this date, or be fired."

There were serious issues with the staple. Those of us who were senior sales people (At 2 ½ years, I was the most tenured sales person in my region. Lots of turnover among the sales force.) had reservations about the safety and efficacy of the product. It didn't matter. The mandatory quotas stood.

I felt that I could not ethically represent the product to the customers who had come to trust me, and so, in spite of tremendous pressure from above, I didn't put any effort into selling it.

I realized that I was putting my job in jeopardy. The situation was building to a climax.

Ah, but it petered out in typical fashion. The regional manager decided to take another job, and there was no one there to enforce the company's latest dictates. The issue blew over, and I was still employed.

But the moral dilemma uncovered by this sequence of events was only the latest in a long string. I began to psychologically remove myself from the company. I couldn't see myself making a career with this organization. I was convinced that somewhere down the road, I'd have to compromise my ethics to stay employed. The indicators were pretty clear.

It was time to find something else.

Chapter Eight

Reflections: The place of integrity in a Christian Salesperson

I was speaking to a group of professional salespeople in Johannesburg, South Africa, on the subject of integrity in business. At dinner later in the evening, my host, who had been sitting in the audience, sheepishly shared with me that several of the people seated near her snickered at the idea. Evidently, to them sales was just a series of transactions, and the salesperson's job was to wring as much money out of each transaction as possible, under whatever means were necessary.

Their position was, I believe, both sad as well as unwise. I believe that there are certainly practices in the business world where morality perfectly coincides with wise business. Integrity is one such practice. It is both good business as well as good morals.

Integrity is both good business as well as good morals.

I believe it is such good business that sales people, especially Christian sales people, should adhere to a no-exceptions policy of maintaining absolute integrity. I'm not going to make the case for absolute honesty as a moral policy. That's better left to our churches

49

to do. There is, however, a powerful case to be made for honesty from a practical point of view.

Honesty is a powerful sales strategy that is probably more important today than ever before.

It works like this. If you have integrity, you save your customer time. In today's frenzied world, time is more precious than money for a lot of people. If your customers cannot believe you, then they must spend hours, days or weeks of precious time confirming the representations you have made. If, however, they can believe you, then they don't feel the need to check for the veracity of every fact or statement.

Here's an illustration. A few years ago, we attempted to purchase a condominium. The condo was in a resort location and had been used as a rental unit. So, it came fully furnished, down to the silverware and cooking utensils. We thought it was a good value, a wise investment, and offered the owner exactly his asking price. Shortly thereafter, word came from the real estate agent that the owner, on receiving our full price offer, had increased his price.

The owner may have been looking at his action as a slick negotiating ploy. We saw it as a lack of integrity. If we couldn't believe his stated price, then we couldn't believe any of the representations he had made. We would be reduced to counting the number of knives and forks instead of believing the inventory sheet provided for us. We didn't want to waste the time checking out every aspect of the deal. If we couldn't trust some of the representations by the owner, then we couldn't trust any. And, if we couldn't trust any, it wasn't worth it to us to take the risk in dealing with him. We walked away from the deal.

We saw the owner's lack of integrity as causing us to invest a great deal of time to assure ourselves that the risk was worth the money.

In this case, we were the buyers who saw the seller's lack of integrity as causing us to spend more time on the project. We chose not to do that.

The same is true of your customers. The more your customer trusts you, the less risk your customer feels in dealing with you, and the less time necessary to invest in understanding the product, service or program you are offering. From the customer's perspective, it's easier and less risky to deal with someone you trust than with someone you don't trust.

From the customer's perspective, it's easier and less risky to deal with someone you trust than with someone you don't trust.

And that can translate directly into dollars. I'm always willing to pay more for something if I can buy it with less risk. In other words, if I can buy it from a company or person I can trust. On the other hand, I'd rather not buy something at all if I have suspicious feelings about the vendor.

Here's another example. A few years ago, I grew jealous of my neighbor's lawn. His was far greener, thicker and fuller than my lawn. It was because he had a lawn care service fertilize his lawn several times each year. I determined to do the same thing. So, I obtained the name and phone number of the company he used, formed an idea of what the service would cost me, and decided to do business with that company.

I called the company, ready to buy the service. When I inquired about the types of service available, the salesperson indicated that there were several options available. Now, I'm a visually oriented person, and I like to make decisions based on what I read, not on what I hear. So, I said, "OK, why not come out and do the first application, and leave me a brochure so that I can review my options, and then I'll make a decision." The salesperson agreed.

We then reviewed the details of my location, and the approximate date for the first fertilizer application. It was a deal. The salesperson then repeated our agreement, saying, "OK, we'll be out to do the first application and we'll leave a brochure, and then you can cancel at any time with 30 days' notice."

"What?" I said.

He repeated his comment. "Wait a minute," I said. "I only agreed to one application. I'm not committing to any ongoing contract until I check out all the options."

"But that's not how we do it," the salesperson stammered.

"No," I said.

"But, But..." more stammers.

"No." I said again. "Forget it. Cancel me."

What happened? Here I was, as good a prospect as there ever was. I was ready to purchase, having decided to use this company, even calling them to make the purchase. Yet something in what the salesperson said raised a red flag in my mind, and made me doubt the integrity of the person, and by inference, the company. He had originally said that I would be billed for only one application, and then implied that I was committing to an ongoing program.

I viewed that as being deceitful, or at best manipulative. If I can't trust them on that, on what can I trust them? There are lots of other lawn care companies, and the next one in the yellow pages got my business.

Life's too short, and business is too busy to deal with people you can't trust. The question, then, for you as a salesperson is this: Do your customers see you as trustworthy?

That's a difficult question to answer. You can't just ask them, because you know you are unlikely to hear a candid response. But you can gain a sense of their perception of you by looking for some of the symptoms of trust or a lack of it.

For example, if you find your customers sometimes buying from a higher priced source or buying a product or service you consider to be inferior, it may be that your customer doesn't trust you!

On the other hand, if you find your customers accepting your word, and choosing to deal with you, even when you are offering an identical product at a higher price, then chances are they do trust you. Your reputation for honesty and integrity has been a smart business strategy, resulting in measurable benefits to you.

Unfortunately, a reputation for trustworthiness and honesty is not a result of one event or a single transaction. It doesn't develop out of some clever phrases you memorize and repeat. Rather, it develops over time as you adhere to a set of ethical standards in small as well as big things. It's not a technique you use, but rather it's the person you chose to become. As you strive to adhere to the standard of absolute honesty and integrity in all that you do, you'll develop a character trait that will become evident to everyone around you, including your customers. And that is good business as well as good morals.

Chapter Nine

On the side

At that time, US Surgical offered the professional sales person the best of a number of situations. The pay plan was 100% commission, and you bought your demo materials and literature from the company. When you converted and trained a surgeon, from then on, every time he used your product you made money. This produced something of an annuity. As you added using surgeons, your income increased.

As salespeople, we all really functioned as independent agents, even though we were company employees. The management did not really care when and where we spent our time, as long as we produced. That kind of environment attracted and retained some of the strongest sales people with whom I had ever been associated. For those of us at the time, we became like a band of brothers – all of us extremely capable sales people, doing this intense sales work and enjoying the rewards of that.

My success at US Surgical had put me to an enviable position. I had converted a number of surgeons who were routinely using the staplers, and that provided a steady and solid income stream.

At the same time, I was beginning to see more clearly how my Christianity interfaced with my job. The Lord had clearly stepped in to energize my success at US Surgical, and I had the conversion of one of my business contacts to reflect upon.

One more piece -- I was beginning to feel more confident and more competent. I had, after all, been exceptionally successful as a sales person. In my days selling men's suits, I was routinely the top performing sales person in the store, and often number one in the entire five store chain. At Jewel Tea, I had won a scholarship as the outstanding college student in my region. I became the number one sales person at HC Electronics, and was enjoying stature and success at US Surgical. Maybe I was pretty good.

So, here I was, feeling pretty good about my abilities, thinking that I could use my business contacts and acumen for the Lord somehow, and given a gift of extra time. It was the perfect time to swing for the fences and take a big risk.

First, a little perspective. I had been a Christian a bit more than five years, and had grown in the faith. I clearly saw that the way to become a "real" Christian was to be involved in the church as a full-time minister of some sort. My interest in becoming a paid, professional minister was always just under the surface. Earlier, I had applied for a number of positions as an educational minister in large congregations. My background and lack of seminary education

were a hindrance. I didn't fit the mold of an ordained "minister," and was rejected everywhere. So, at this point, I saw myself, as far as the church went, as being a bit outside of the conventional, and something of a misfit.

It was a constant frustration. I had all this education, these developing skills which the business world obviously valued, but no place in the church. Oh, I was allowed to pass the communion tray, and occasionally lead a prayer, or even teach a class, but there was no place where I could use my education and skills. I was becoming resigned to being a second class Christian.

If I was going to be active in the church, at a level where I could use my talents, then I was going to have to do it in a different way.

I saw a big need in the church. Sunday school teachers were well-intentioned volunteers, but who had no idea of how to teach. That was a need I could fill. With my educational background, and what I'd learned from the US Surgical seminars, I could teach them how to teach. So, I created a course for Sunday school teachers called "How to Use Dynamics in the Bible School." It was a course in teaching techniques, designed for the average Sunday school teacher.

I taught it in person in a couple of churches, and it was warmly received. I had a winner.

Now, with my evolving confidence, my extra time, my growing insight into the relationship of the Lord in my life, and my deep desire to do something of significant in the church, I decided to form a business and promote the program nation-wide.

I convinced a few other people to invest in the idea (including one of my surgeon-customers) and created Christian Dynamics, Inc. Our purpose was to take my "How to Use Dynamics" course and put it into duplicable form.

As strange as it may sound, video technology was just getting off the ground. I saw it as the perfect medium to duplicate my course. I contracted with the video department of a local college, and video-taped the lessons. Then I created "student's guides' for the teachers who would take the course, and a "leader's guide" for whoever would be leading the course in the local church.

The technology was so new that home video players were almost non-existent. I bought a number of big, heavy commercial video players, had special shipping cases built for them, and would rent them to the congregations who bought the course.

Now, I was ready to go with a state-of-the-art training program, using the latest technologies, addressing one of the greatest needs in the church. This may have been the first multi-session, multi-media video training courses available anywhere — Christian or otherwise. It was a sure winner and would provide me with the vehicle to spend all my time in "full-time ministry."

I marketed it with every bit of know how I had. Full color brochures, direct mail letters to targeted lists, advertisements in the appropriate publications, etc.

At that time, regional Christian conferences were the rage, and I booked space in a half dozen, had a booth designed, and flew off to exhibit and show the system face to face with the movers and shakers of the institutional church.

Over the next couple of years, I sold maybe a half dozen courses. The overwhelming response from the church was indifference. Many pastors saw me as a threat. I'm sure many of them thought that if they bought the course, that meant that they were not able to teach it. It somehow diminished their stature. And if some of their volunteer teachers became good at teaching, that might in some way threaten the pastor's stature. The most common objection was "we can do that ourselves." Never mind that they never had, never did, and never would.

I'd easily find interested teachers, and they would take the proposal back to their pastors and elders, where it routinely died.

I had a great product, but the decision makers didn't want it. Once again, it was clear to me that I wasn't good enough to have an impact for the Lord.

Then, in one of the regional conferences, an older gentleman wandered into the booth and saw, immediately, the power and potential of the product. It turned out he was one of the most well-known, well-respected itinerant ministers of that denomination. He had a large mail order Christian book store, and traveled all over the country, speaking to large groups. Would I be interested in merging the companies, he wanted to know, and let him use his credibility and visibility to promote the program?

The Lord had stepped in, at last. This was the perfect solution. His credibility was such that if he recommended it, the churches would line up to buy it. My sales problem was solved!

He put me into contact with the manager of the store. We quickly became friends and we pushed the logistics forward. I traveled to Tulsa, OK, where his operation was located, stayed at the older gentleman's house, and looked for a home to buy, as we would be moving.

I put my home up for sale and prepared for my new life as a trainer of Sunday school teachers. It was an exciting time.

Before I was about to sign an offer on a home in Tulsa, I needed a document from him to verify my income and qualify for a mortgage. He didn't return the phone call. In fact, he never returned another phone call. Nor did his manager. It was I had suddenly dropped off the face of the earth and ceased to exist.

After two weeks of leaving feverish messages, I finally got it. The merger wasn't going to happen. For whatever reason, he had changed his mind, and didn't have the courage to say it to me face-to-face.

What a disappointment. All this time and effort going to waste. It was a great product, perfect for a huge need, and no one was interested. In addition,

one of the most highly respected paragons of the faith turned out to be spineless and unreliable. It was like someone had hit me in the stomach with a baseball bat. What a defeat. I could hardly breathe.

And I couldn't understand the Lord allowing this to happen. It was His church. He saw the need. How could He have let this happen? I was confused, frustrated, and defeated.

There was no more money left in the company. My paychecks from US Surgical had ended. I needed to get a job.

Chapter Ten

Reflections on The Role of Adversity in Shaping a Sales Person's Character

I still remember the worst sales call I ever made – that horribly embarrassing moment at the Detroit Public Schools. More than just remember it, I react to the memory. I get a queasy feeling in my stomach every time I think about it. It wasn't just a bad sales call, it was a humiliating, embarrassing event. I don't think I'll ever forget it.

That's the point. There is something about adversity that has the power to linger forever in our memories, shaping our character and molding our behavior for the rest of our life.

Adversity can take countless forms. It can be a gut-wrenching incident, like my worst sales call, or more poignantly, something like an auto accident or the loss of a loved one. I've had them all. Or, it can be a period of financial distress – yes, I've had that too, a couple of times. Or, it can be a time of health problems, and relationship conflicts. Yep, you guessed it. I've lived through both of those situations as well.

Regardless, the Encarta Dictionary defines adversity this way:

1. misfortune (hardship and suffering)

2. adverse happening (an extremely unfavorable experience or event)

One of the things that these experiences have in common is their impact on us – they create an intense, negative emotional response. We become angry, embarrassed, humiliated, depressed, and hopeless. Adversity produces a grab-bag of bad feelings. It's not fun. As I reflect on my personal experiences, I have to acknowledge that the events mentioned above were some of the worst hours, days, and months of my life. I never want to go through any of them again.

But it is that intensity of emotional response that contains the seeds that can bloom into a sounder character, if we respond appropriately. We've all heard the expression, "What doesn't kill us makes us stronger." Sort of true, but not exactly. That common expression would be more accurate if we tacked on the phrase, "if we let it." The real truth is: "What doesn't kill us makes us stronger, if we let it."

What doesn't kill us makes us stronger, if we let it.

"If we let it," is the secret. There's no guarantee that, by itself, without our active and appropriate response, adversity will make us stronger. I've met, and I'm sure you have too, many people who allowed adversity to turn them into bitter or defeated individuals. To them, life is a burden, the world is a dangerous place, and they can't do much about it. It's easy, and tempting, to allow adversity to fester into a "victim mentality" in us.

In order to prevent that from happening, in order to grow "stronger," we must learn from those painful experiences. And, in learning, we create habits that emerge as character traits, and thus we become better and more capable people.

My humiliating sales call, for example, taught me a simple lesson that has stuck with me for decades and has flowered into a broader character trait. "Never speak badly about the competition" was the lesson. I like to think that "Respect for all my competitors" is the broader character trait. The periods of financial hardship have developed an empathy in me for those in similar circumstances, and a very conservative financial perspective. The death of my daughter is somehow pushing up buds of greater patience, empathy and tolerance in my character.

While I never want to go through any of these things again, I am probably a better person because of them -- and because of my response to them.

In the long run, it is what you do with your response to adversity that will make all the difference.

Here are a couple of practical suggestions to help you deal with your adversity:

Take the high road.

Don't allow the circumstances to drag you down, to compromise your values, or impinge on your relationships. I had a renter, for example, in a house that we own. He was laid off from his job. Instead of being honest about it, he made up stories, told lies, and eventually stuck me with two months unpaid rent and damages to the house. While I have to deal with the financial damages, he has a significantly diminished character. Because he took the low road, he's less of a man today than he was before.

Don't give into the temptation to take ethical short-cuts or to abandon your responsibilities. Take the high road.

Learn from it.

At some point, you'll have an opportunity to look on your adverse circumstances somewhat objectively. That's when you'll want to ask yourself this question: "What can I learn from this?" Then follow up with a more pointed version of this question, "What can I do differently, as a result of what I've learned?"

Ask, "What can I do differently, as a result of what I've learned?"

The answer to "What can I learn from my embarrassing sales call" was, "Customers don't like to hear you talk badly about a competing product or person." That would be academic information if I didn't follow up with the second question: "What can I do differently, as a result of what I've learned?" The answer to that question was, "Never speak badly about a competitor."

The emphasis must eventually rest on us and our response. If we don't change anything we do, believe, or think, then we will have learned nothing.

Eventually we must change what we do. That's the key to growing from adversity. As long as we focus on other people or our circumstances, we'll be forever locked in a victim mentality. Remember, "if we let it."

Our Creator put us on this earth to grow, develop and become more like Him. Adversity is the fertilizer that stimulates that growth, if we let it.

At some point, this will pass. At that point, the real measure of this set of circumstances will be the impact on your character.

Chapter Eleven

Head hunting

There I was -- unemployed, frustrated, defeated, and out of money. And, I had a family to support. So, I registered with a couple of employment agencies that specialized in placing sales people. They both offered me a job working for them. In my precarious financial situation, I needed an income as soon as possible.

I wasn't sure about the job, but both of them seemed to think that I could do it, so I accepted one of the offers, and went to work for Greening-Hoffman, as a head-hunter, specializing in placing sales people.

Like US Surgical, it was a 100% commission job, with a six-month draw. As a sales recruiter, I learned to work both sides of the hiring decision. Place an ad in the newspaper for a sales person, then interview and collect resumes of the sales people who replied, hoping to find one or two good candidates. Equipped with those applications, I'd pitch them to local sales managers of companies who likely could use them. I'd get a job order from the sales manager, and advertise it, repeating the cycle.

I didn't like it. First, it was 9 – 5 in an office, every day. It had been years since I went to a place of employment, having worked out of my home my entire sales career. I found the routine stifling. In addition, it became clear that success in this business was purely a matter of numbers. In other words, for every five or six interviews you set up, you'd get one placement and one commission. It didn't matter how conscientious you were at the job, trying to ferret out exactly what the manager was looking for and trying to find exactly the right fit. The numbers were the numbers.

Do a great job, and you placed one out of six interviews. Do a poor job, and you placed one out of six interviews. Do a mediocre job, and you placed one out of six interviews. I quickly caught on -- to make more money, arrange more interviews.

What sounded like a professional sales position turned out to be a telemarketing position, and the most successful recruiters pounded the phone relentlessly. While I didn't like this work, I gained some important understandings and skills. I learned, for example, that there were some basic career paths for someone intent on a career in sales. If you wanted to climb the corporate ladder, and become a vice-president 20 years from now, you applied to a certain type of company. If you wanted to make a lot of money, but burn out in a couple of years, there were companies who offered that.

I learned the skill of interviewing, and particularly interviewing sales people. That was later to become one of the services I offered as a sales consultant, and the experience I gained recruiting sales people provided the raw material for my first multi-media program.

After about a year, I decided this wasn't for me. Time, once again, to look for another job.

This time, I had the luxury of being employed while I looked for another job. I could take my time and be selective. So, I thought carefully about what I wanted. First, I wanted to go with a company that offered me the opportunity to fashion a career – or at least a long-term job. I wanted to settle in for a while.

Secondly, I wanted a place where I could make good money. I thought I was pretty good as a salesman, and I didn't want my income to be limited. That meant a 100% commission compensation program.

Third, I wanted a variety of things to sell. Part of my restlessness with Phonic Ear had to do with the limited product line. I just got bored.

Fourth, I had a family at home, and I didn't want to travel much. So, limited overnight travel was my fourth requirement. Finally, I wanted a company with some integrity.

As I talked to sales people and sales managers at the agency, I filtered the conversation through those filters. Eventually, I came down to two companies. I went to both, telling them about my criteria, my interest in their company, and desire to go to work for them. "If ever you are looking for a sales person," I told them both, "I'd like for you to consider me, as I'd like to work for you."

They both did.

The story of how I wound up with one instead of the other is a great example of how the Lord worked this out. I interviewed with both companies. The first, on Thursday, offered me the job. I told them I was interviewing with the other company as well and expected to receive a job offer from them. My plan was to consider both over the weekend and make my decision by Monday morning. That was acceptable to the first company.

On Friday, I interviewed with the second company, a hospital supply distributor called White & White. The interview was at the Northfield Hilton Hotel, in the western suburbs of Detroit. Ned, the branch manager with whom I was interviewing, offered me the job. I said the same thing to him that I had said to the first company. That was OK with Ned.

It was now about 5 PM on Friday afternoon, and Ned suggested that we share a beer before we headed home. So, we settled into a table in the lounge, and ordered a couple of draft beers.

The door to a meeting room opened, no more than 15 feet from where we were sitting. Out came the VP of the first company – the one I had interviewed with the previous day. It turns out they were having a sales meeting in the same hotel. He saw me sitting there with Ned and came up and chatted for a few minutes and then left.

Over the weekend I decided to take the first company's offer. First thing Monday morning, I called him and told him of my decision. "I'm afraid we can't hire you," the VP said. "When I saw you and Ned sitting there Friday afternoon, Ned looked so pleased with himself that I figured that you had accepted his offer. So, on Saturday morning, I spoke with the President, and we decided to divide the territory we were going to give to you up among the existing sales people. So, there isn't an open territory. I'm sorry."

"That's OK," I said. Then I called Ned and told him that I had decided to take his offer.

A few years later, I looked back on this and saw the Lord arranging circumstances to put me into White & White, which was the launching pad for my next career.

The Lord arranged circumstances to put me into White & White, which was the launching pad for my next career.

The Greening-Hoffman experience was a great learning experience. I learned that I wasn't invulnerable. My performance there was mediocre. I was not a success. My temperament, skills and talents were just not suited to the demands of that job.

I was beginning to see the borders around the types of things I could be good at, and those from which I should stay away. I liked the complex sale, where strategy and thoughtfulness were required to pull off a deal. I was good at highly technical products where my knowledge was critical to the sale, and miserable at regular maintenance and repetitious tasks. To this day, I have trouble doing something in the same way twice.

I was beginning to understand a powerful rule of success – you are much more likely to be successful if you are in a situation where your strengths and talents fit the demands of the situation. If what you are good at is what the job requires, you will be successful. If not, it will be a struggle.

In my next job, I was a great fit.

Lesson learned: You are much more likely to be successful if you are in a situation where your strengths and talents fit the demands of the situation.

Chapter Twelve

Reflections: The Ultimate Success Skill

In the last 12 months, only one out of every 20 sales people have spent $25.00 or more on their own improvement! Incredible. Let me repeat it to make sure you read it correctly: In the last 12 months, only one out of every 20 sales people have spent $25.00 or more of their own money on their own improvement! That's my conclusion, based on lots of anecdotal evidence collected over the past 25 years of working with sales people.

I am embarrassed by that. Only five percent of my colleagues are sufficiently dedicated to their own personal growth and professional success that they will invest their own money in their careers. That means that ninety-five percent are not sufficiently motivated to take their own personal development seriously. What a shame.

Only five percent of sales people are sufficiently dedicated to their own personal growth and professional success that they will invest their own money in their own careers.

I am convinced that the process of continuously improving – not only professionally in the core competencies of a professional sales person, but also personally as well – is the ultimate success skill for our time.

The ability to learn and grow in a proactive and disciplined way is several things:

1. A method to do better at your job. Good sales people sell more than mediocre sales people. Good sales people make more money, enjoy more success and greater status than mediocre sales people. Good sales people work at becoming better.

2. A way to distinguish yourself from the masses. Remember, ninety-five percent of your competitors and colleagues don't care enough to invest in themselves. When you do that, you eventually separate yourself from the pack.

3. A minimal requirement for your employer. I often tell my clients that every sales person (and every employee, for that matter) has two jobs:

   a. his job, and

   b. continually improving himself. If someone is not interested in improving his skills, I don't want him working for me, or for my clients.

4. An ethical imperative. It is, I believe, immoral to not improve yourself. Your employer has hired you not just for what you know and what you can do, but for your potential to know more and do more. When you refuse to improve yourself, you rob your employer of some of the reasons he pays you. That, to me, is immoral.

When you refuse to improve yourself, you rob your employer of some of the reasons he pays you.

The same is true for your family, friends and people with whom you have some influence. You owe it to them to become the best that you can become.

5. A necessary process that inevitably leads to spiritual growth. Spiritual growth is, of course, "growth." Growth requires positive change and transformation. Thus, the ability to grow and change in a dedicated and disciplined way is a requirement for serious spiritual growth. Additionally, a serious student of personal improvement inevitably moves from focus on tactical issues to deeper, more spiritual, issues.

That's a lot of value wrapped up in a single, fundamental process. You can see why I believe that the ability to learn in a focused, systematic way is the ultimate competency -- the foundational skill that, if mastered, will eventually lead you to success.

I call this -- the ultimate self-improvement skill for turbulent times and beyond -- "self-directed learning."

When you hear the word *learning* you're probably reminded of your days in school, or perhaps seminars and company-sponsored training programs come to mind. While these are all means of facilitating learning, they don't capture the essence of the ultimate success skill.

Self-directed learning is the ability of individuals to absorb new information and to change their behavior in positive ways in response. The key is behavior change. Learning without action is impotent. Knowledge that doesn't result in changed action is of little value. Constantly changing your behavior in positive ways is the only reasonable response to a constantly changing world.

For example, let's say that you've read my book, _Question Your Way to Sales Success_. That's a necessary first step. But, it's one thing to read and understand the material in the book, and it's another to actually use it. It's nice that you understand it, and it's good that you think it may help you. But that particular piece of information is worthless until you actually start using it. When you change your behavior and incorporate those ideas into what you do, then you will have learned. Everything else – the reading, understanding, and mental processing that came first – is necessary but not sufficient. They, by themselves, fall short of the goal. It is not until you actually do that new thing – ask questions more effectively, that you will have learned.

Self-directed learning differs from the traditional approaches to training

because it requires you to assume complete responsibility for your own behavior change. The stimulus for the learning must come from within you. You must take the initiative to expose yourself to new ideas, and then to change your behavior in positive ways as a result.

You must take the initiative to expose yourself to new ideas, and then to change your behavior in positive ways as a result.

In every direction to which you look, you're faced with rapid changes. And these changes require you, if you're going to stay competitive, to learn and change at a rate never before required of you.

I firmly believe that the ability to take charge of your own learning, to consistently expose yourself to new information, and then to systematically change your behavior in positive ways based on that new information is the *ultimate* success skill for the Information Age.

If you can master self-directed learning, you'll eventually master everything else that you need to be successful.

Prerequisites to Mastering Self-Directed Learning

Proficiency at the ultimate self-improvement skill demands some fundamental attitudes on your part. I like to characterize those attitudes as being a "seeker."

A seeker attitude is composed of several parts. First, you must have an attitude of proactive responsibility for your situation. In other words, you must believe that your actions have consequences and that to change the consequences, you must change your actions.

You must believe that your actions have consequences and that to change the consequences, you must change your actions.

This sounds so fundamental as to be ludicrous, yet it seems to be a concept that is foreign to much of the world's population. Most people tend to blame their problems on forces outside themselves. Your parents didn't raise you correctly, your spouse doesn't understand you, your boss doesn't like you, your customers don't respect you, the stars are aligned against you, etc. As long as you remain, in your mind, the victim of someone else or some outside force, you have no responsibility to change your own behavior. After all, your situation isn't your fault.

That's exactly the wrong attitude. If you are going to be successful, you'll need to begin with the conviction that your actions have consequences, and that you can change your future. Once you get that, then you are ready to discover what actions will have the greatest impact on your success.

So, you must accept the responsibility for your *own* behavior as well as for the consequence of that behavior. As one of my clients said to me, "If you always do what you always did, you'll always get what you always got."

**If you always do what you always did,
you'll always get what you always got.**

That's common sense. But think about the implications of that statement. If you want different results, you must do something differently in order to get them. The emphasis is on *do.* The responsibility is yours.

Next, sales people with a seeker attitude need to be open to new information. One of the sure harbingers of pending failure is the attitude that you know it all. Sales people who continue to improve themselves understand that they will never have *all* the answers. There is *always* something new to learn. They become like magnets, constantly attracting new ideas, new perspectives, and new information to themselves.

Finally, a seeker has the ability to follow through on his plans. *You* must have the ability to act on decisions you make, and to become a creature whose actions arise out of conscious thought rather than unconscious habit. In other words, you must have the strength to decide to do something and then to follow through with that decision and actually do it.

From time to time, people ask me about the characteristics of my clients. They're expecting me to answer with the size of various companies, or how many sales people they have, or the product lines they serve. They're always surprised when I answer that my clients are not defined by size or products.

Rather, they are defined by the personality of the Chief Executive Officer (CEO). All of my clients have CEOs who are open minded, interested in outside perspectives, willing to learn, and committed to the growth of their businesses. The sales people who attend my seminars can be described with the same terms. They're seekers.

It's interesting that this description only applies to a small percentage of the population. It probably describes you, or you wouldn't be reading this E-zine. Take heart in that. In a rapidly-changing world, the competent, self-directed learners will end up on top. The fact that you're probably one of them means that you're already separating yourself from the mass of distributor sales people who are more interested in maintaining the status quo.

Richard Gaylord Briley, in his book *Everything I Needed to Know about Success I Learned in the Bible,* talks about the five percent principle. You're familiar with the Pareto Principle -- the 80/20 rule. Applied to sales, the principle says that 20 percent of your customers provide 80 percent of your business, and that 20 percent of the sales people capture 80 percent of the business. Briley's five percent rule is similar. It holds that five percent of the individuals in the world provide success and opportunity for 50 percent of the rest of the population. Applied to sales, the Briley rule would hold that five percent of the sales people in the world contribute 50 percent of the volume.

I believe that these five percenters are active, self-directed learners who maintain the seeker attitude I've described. And I believe that *you* have the potential to be a five-percenter for the rest of your life. The starting point is the cultivation of the seeker attitude.

Given this set of attitudes, you can begin to master the procedures and disciplines that will characterize you as a self-directed learner and equip you to be successful in our turbulent times.

Core Strategies for Self-Directed Learning

If you have the right attitude, you'll find the following two strategies to be powerful ways to practice self-directed learning.

1. Inject yourself into learning opportunities.

There are two parts to the learning equation. The first is to constantly expose yourself to new information, and the second is to change your behavior in positive ways based on that information.

For example, reading this book is a way to expose yourself to new information. So is listening to a podcast or CD, attending a seminar, etc. That's the first half of the process. If you now make changes in what you do as a result of it, you've accomplished the second half.

The second part rarely happens unless the first part precedes it. So, to put the whole process into motion, you must regularly expose yourself to new information. To do that, you must inject yourself into learning opportunities. You're thinking, "What's a learning opportunity?" It's any event or situation that causes you to face some new information, or that stimulates you to reformat information you already have.

Here are a number of ways to inject yourself into learning opportunities that will help you continuously improve.

Read books, magazines and newsletters. I'm often asked to recommend a book for a new sales person to read. I usually respond by suggesting that, after they have read all of my books, they go to the library and check out anything that looks interesting. While clearly my books are the best ever written, if your attitude is right, you can learn from anything. So, in one sense, it doesn't make any difference what you expose yourself to, as long as you expose yourself to *something*.

Reading any book is better than reading no book. With the proliferation of business books available these days, you can go to the local bookstore or library every couple of weeks and find new books to read. Almost any book you can find will give you new ideas or, at the least, new ways of reformulating things you already know in more useful and practical ways.

In addition to reading books regularly, subscribe to one or more of the sales magazines or newsletters. They make a point of discussing the latest thoughts and presenting contemporary sales situations. There are a number of good magazines and newsletters available.

Make use of podcasts and CDs on sales techniques. These media have the advantage of allowing you to put drive time to good use. Just pop a CD or an MP3 file on your I-pod into the player between calls, and you'll be amazed at how many good ideas you can get.

Many of my clients have created lending libraries of CDs. The company owns dozens of programs, and sales people check them out one at a time, and return them when they're done. You'll find lots of these kinds of resources on my on-line web site: www.thesalesresourcecenter.com. Listening to CDs and podcasts is a way of continually exposing yourself to a powerful body of new information

Attend seminars and workshops. Seminars and workshops provide you an opportunity to meet with other sales people and see things from a different point of view -- not to mention the material and ideas you garner from the seminar leader.

In some locations, you may have the opportunity to join a learning group. We have organized and facilitated a number of these locally. We bring a dozen or so sales people or CEOs together for a two-hour meeting in which we discuss an aspect of sales in detail. The idea is to learn from one another by engaging in a focused, facilitated discussion group.

Make use of DVDs and online learning programs. Our economy is awash with programs of all kinds. In an hour's concentrated work, you could probably identify thousands of possible DVDs, CDs and online programs. Visit our Sales Resource Center ® for an on-line portal with over 450 training programs for sales people and sales leaders.

Whether you use our materials or someone else's, the important thing is that you use something!

Add these technique and personal self-improvement learning situations to your normal product learning opportunities, and you get an idea of the kind of learning commitment you need to make in order to seriously and continually transform yourself.

Remember that it's not enough to go to a seminar once a year or read a book every now and then. Learning should be a regular part of your work week. I'd like to see you do something to exposure yourself to new ideas every week.

Reflect on your failures. You're probably thinking, "Where did that come from?" I have learned that *my* failures, both as a sales person and in my life in general, have provided me with my most intensive learning experiences. In fact, I remember all my failures far more vividly than I remember any of my successes. As I thought about each one of them, I discovered what I had done to produce that failure, and I made specific decisions to change to prevent them from happening again.

Personally, I think that this practice has been one of the key reasons for the success that I have enjoyed as a sales person. You can do the same thing. You are going to fail from time to time. Everyone does. The most important part of failing is taking the time to reflect on the failure and to learn from it.

Be sensitive to all your failures, large or small, and take the time to reflect on them. You'll find them to be potent learning experiences.

2. Question everything.

There are two big obstacles to learning that are especially typical of sales people. The first is "stuck in a rut" behavior. The second is the tendency to over-rely on assumptions. The cure for both is the same: to question everything.

Stuck in a rut behavior evolves out of an attitude that you already know enough. If you're content and smug about your current situation, you're not going to be open to new information. This satisfaction hinders learning because it hampers the motivation to learn. Without the motivation to expose yourself to new information and seriously consider changing your behavior, the necessary changes won't happen. You're stuck in the status quo -- oblivious to the need to move out of it.

One of the best ways to pry yourself out of a rut is to begin to ask yourself questions. Question everything you do. Is this the best way to present this product? Should you be calling on this customer once a week? Are you presenting the right solutions? Do you really know your customers as well as you should?

Got the idea? The starting point for getting out of the rut behavior is to prod yourself via pointed questions.

The other major obstacle to learning is the tendency to do your job based on unchallenged assumptions. This occurs when you operate on the basis of an assumption that you've never really thought about. For example, you assume that two or three competitors are quoting the same piece of business you are, so you discount deeply. Or, you assume that your customers always know exactly what they want, so you don't take the time to question them.

Unchallenged assumptions cause errors. Because you work on an assumption instead of taking the time to verify it, you make decisions that are inappropriate.

The solution is the same as getting out of a rut. Question everything. From time to time, stop and ask yourself what assumptions you're working on, and then question those assumptions. You'll often find that your assumptions are in error, and the decisions you made that relied on them were also in error.

Chapter Thirteen

White & White

White & White was a large regional distributor of medical and surgical products to both hospitals and doctor's offices. That meant that they bought from all the established manufacturers, names like Johnson & Johnson, Kimberly Clark, Bard, etc., inventoried those items, and resold them to their customers -- hospitals and doctor's offices throughout the state of Michigan. At the time, they had 40,000 items on their price list and many of those in stock.

I was given a sales territory comprised of 77 hospitals in a pie-slice shaped territory that began in downtown Detroit, and extended northward through the "thumb" of Michigan. It was a new territory, with just a few thousands of dollars of existing business. The company, which was headquartered in Grand Rapids, Michigan, had just purchased a distributor on the east side of the state, and made that their Detroit-area branch. I was the first new sales person hired in that new branch.

The selling situation was considerably different than that which I had experienced in the past. At Jewel Tea, Phonic Ear, and US Surgical, I had a product that was unique and brought specific benefits to the customer. With White & White, I had 40,000 products and most of those could be purchased from a competitor as well. With the

89

exception of a small group of exclusive or semi-exclusive lines, the product wasn't the primary issue in the mind of my customer.

Take for example, a simple Band-Aid, made by someone like Johnson & Johnson. J&J did not want to sell boxes of band aids to tens of thousands of hospitals directly, as it was too costly. So, they sold to distributors, like White & White, in large quantities. The local distributors then warehoused and sold directly to the hospitals in the quantities that they wanted. Since the local distributor handled hundreds of lines, and thousands of products, the sales cost for the band aid was spread over all those products, and thus reduced to next to nothing.

The hospital could buy their band aids and well as their surgical gloves, disposable shoe coverings, needles and syringes, etc. from someone who warehoused them locally and could provide them quickly.

White & White was a great example of the notorious "middle man," but one which served a valuable function both for the manufacturers as well as the hospital customers.

The manufacturers were able to ship in large quantities to fewer customers, reducing their costs of receivables, shipping, etc. Also, since the distributor sales people provided the interface with the customer, the manufacturers didn't need to have lots of sales people calling on every hospital, thereby reducing their sales costs dramatically.

The customers could consolidate their orders, and instead of buying one box from each of 50 different suppliers, could buy 50 boxes from one, thereby reducing their purchasing costs. Since the distributors were typically within a day's delivery, the hospitals could run on minimal inventories, again reducing their inventory costs.

The middle man provided a win-win option for everyone.

This was an entirely different sales challenge than I was accustomed to.

Hospitals would choose to buy for a number of reasons. The relationship with the sales person and the company was very important. If they were comfortable with you, liked you, and trusted you, that, in many cases, was enough.

In a world where they could buy the same products from three or four other vendors, price became important, as did delivery. If you warehoused the product, and delivered twice a week, you had the advantage over your competitor who may not have as great a supply on hand and deliver only once a week.

Once a hospital decided to buy a certain product or line from you, the purchasing department would issue a purchase order for a period of time, say six months or a year, and you would have the security of knowing that you had that business. Success as a salesperson was in building up the business with multiple product and product lines.

I soon learned to distinguish between those products that we distributed and those that we sold. We distributed name brand products that were carried by other distributors as well. That meant that it just wasn't worth my time to put in any effort to sell that product. If a customer wanted to buy it, I'd supply it to them. It really didn't make any difference to me if they bought brand A or brand B, as long as they bought it from me. With this class of products, I had to give them other reasons to buy from me. That meant price, of course, but also reliable delivery, ease of doing business, great service, and a solid personal relationship.

In additional to those products that we distributed, there were those that we sold. These were exclusive or semi-exclusive lines that generally brought higher margins, required our time to promote, and had the feature that if you could get the customer using it, you would probably maintain the business, as these were generally exclusive or semi-exclusive lines and no other competitor could discount it out from under you.

While there were always requisition items that were purchased on a one-time only basis, almost every sale was contractual, in that the customer agreed to purchase it for an extended period of time. So, you didn't sell a syringe, for example. You sold that line of syringes for a year or two.

This meant that as you acquired a piece of business, you could count on that for at least six months, and more likely a year or more. Your accumulated sales grew as you added new deals to the old ones.

It took me a few months to figure the business out and begin to adjust to this new style of selling. I grew to love it. I loved all the "balls in the air". There could be a dozen different projects going on at any one time in any one account.

Multiply that times the number of accounts, the number of decision makers in each account, the number of manufacturers and lines and sales reps, and it made for a complex mix that I found challenging and exhilarating.

I started out with a minimal amount of business, and was paid a basic, starting salary. Within a year, though, I had grown the business sufficiently to go on 100% commission and spent the next four years seeing an almost monthly increase in my income.

The salesperson's challenge was first and foremost, to manage the customer relationships. Since you saw the same people over and over again, you needed to maintain and manage long-term, constantly growing relationships. In some cases, you would see the same person, at the same time, every week. You had to wear well.

In some of the larger hospitals, there could be three or four people in the purchasing department, and 15 -20 department supervisors of the key departments. Keeping all that straight was a management issue. Deciding who to invest your time in was always a strategic decision.

In addition, the manufacturers whose products we sold and distributed had their own sales reps, who were constantly wanting to spend time with you in an attempt to influence you to sell more of their products.

At the same time, the product side of the job presented similar challenges. With at least 40,000 products, the choice of which of those to spotlight and promote was also a constant challenge.

This called for a lot of thoughtfulness, and constant prioritization and planning. Those demands struck to the heart of my strengths, and I learned to excel at them.

I understood that I needed to create positive business relationships with all my customers and gave that some deep thought. My wife, Coleen, is a gourmet cook, and during this time completed her degree in Culinary Arts. We decided to make use of that talent and create an enormous variety of Christmas cookies and candy. Coleen would start in October, making and freezing the various concoctions. Near Christmas, I would get disposable plastic bed pans, and we would fill them with a cornucopia of treats, wrap them in colored cellophane, and bring them into my customers as Christmas gifts. People soon began to lobby for them, and the project became one of my trade marks. Compared to the cans of nuts and popcorn that my competitors brought in, I was the hit of the season. It became a conversation point all year long, and my customers would make sure they were in the hospital on the day I was scheduled to appear with them.

I happened onto the strategy of entertaining customers, and that became one of the best things I did. During the summer, I would organize outings that always included two customers and their spouses, myself and Coleen, and one manufacturer's rep and his/her spouse. We would have dinner at Greek Town in Detroit, and then do a Tiger game together. I would pay for the entire evening, and the only rule we had was "No one talks business."

Entertaining customers was one of the best things I did.

The good will and closer relationships that these evenings generated always returned economic benefits. Predictably, the next time I saw those customers that I had treated to the baseball outings, they had prepared some additional opportunities for me, and we always expanded the business.

The closer relationships that resulted always brought an economic return.

Several great stories emerged from these occasions. Here's one. I tried to be very strategic with my invitations. In other words, I didn't invite my friends, or the people with who I was comfortable, I would invite those who were strategically most important. One such person was the material manager at a good sized "B" account. He was a crusty, abrasive, ornery guy, and most sales people avoided calling on him. He was, however, the key decision maker in this account, and therefore strategically important. I invited him and his wife to a baseball game outings and he accepted.

The game ended early that night, and we found ourselves at loose ends around 9:30 PM. He suggested that the night was still young, and I volunteered to lead the group to the Woodbridge Tavern, a fun place with Dixie land jazz and peanut shells on the floor. Most of the party declined, but Bill (not his name) and his spouse decided to join us. So, the party of eight became a party of four, and off we went to the Woodbridge.

A couple of beers there, and it really was time to go. My wife and I walked them to their car, which was parked along the curb. Bill went around to open the driver's side door, and I opened the passenger's door for his wife. She started to slide in, stopped, and reached up and hugged me. There were tears in her eyes. She whispered in my ear. "Thank you. No one has ever done this for him before. It means so much to me." And then slid back into her seat.

As a post-script to this story, I should mention that over the next few years I became the number one vendor in that hospital and enjoyed a greater penetration of that account than any other account I had.

Probably one of the most unique strategies that I happened upon was that of managing the manufacturer's reps.

With 40,000 line items, we dealt with hundreds of different manufacturers. Most of them had representatives and they would frequently call and want to work with us, to educate us in their product lines, and encourage us to give time to their lines.

Most distributor sales people looked at this as in imposition and a drag on their routines. I chose to see it as an opportunity.

I choose to be strategic about working with them. Creating a set of criteria, I applied that to the reps themselves as well as to their lines, and identified a set of about 6 – 8 reps whose personalities, skill sets and product lines held the greatest potential. I decided to treat them as customers and influence them to spend time in my territory. The usual approach was to make joint calls together. I reasoned that it didn't make sense for two people to make one call, when two people could make two calls. So, I developed relationships with them, took them to lunch, (and the baseball outings) and got to know their spouses.

I would call them in the evening, pass on a lead and ask them to pursue it and get back to me. Within a short time, I was on the phone with each of them weekly. In a sense, I was managing them. The results were extraordinary. For example, for one of my primary lines, the manufacturer's rep became the number one sales person in the country for her line (out of about 300 reps) and my territory sold more of that line than any other distribution territory in the country.

In that industry, at that time, a million and half dollar territory was the dividing line between those who were striving to succeed and those who had. I began with a territory of approximately $10,000, and, in five years, increased it to $5 Million. That made me the number one sales person in the company, and I was recognized with the "Salesperson of the year" award. The award was made at a formal, black-tie, occasion, with all the men in tuxedos and the women in evening gowns. I still treasure the pictures from that occasion.

I thrived in this selling situation. I enjoyed the multiple possibilities, the challenge to manage hundreds of opportunities and relationships, to constantly strategize and prioritize. Much of the content for several of my books, including *Eleven Secrets of Time Management for Salespeople*, and *How to Excel at Distributor Sales*, had its inception in the days with White and White.

Ned Shaheen, the manager who hired and managed me for most of that time, said to me, "Dave, you should write the book on distributor sales." Later, I did, (*How to Excel at Distributor Sales*) and dedicated it to Ned.

In terms of my relationship with the Lord, I understood that I was a Christian, but I defined that primarily in what I did in church and didn't do on the job. For example, I tried to act with integrity and honesty. I tried to be fair. I would avoid off-color jokes and coarse language. At company meetings, I would be the only one asked to offer a beginning prayer. I found it odd that the company, evidently, could find no one else other than me to pray out loud.

I continued to define Christianity as primarily involved with the church. We went every Sunday and Wednesday and took the kids to all the functions of the church. I taught the adult Sunday school bible class. I think my view was that a good Christian was active in the church, and that the degree to which you were involved with the programs of the local church somehow indicated the depth of your spirituality. People who didn't get involved in the church were not really committed Christians, or so I thought at the time.

There were a couple of church-related incidents that began to set the stage for my movement away from that position. In my Sunday school class, we came across Colossians.3: 22-24:

"Slaves, obey your masters in all things. Do not obey just when they are watching you, to gain their favor, but serve them honestly, because you respect the Lord. In all the work you are doing, work the best you can. Work as if you were doing it for the Lord, not for people. Remember that you will receive your reward from the Lord

98

which He promised to his people. "(Everyday Version, New Century Bible.)

I held the opinion that it meant just what it said. That the modern day application was that you were to give your employer an honest day's work. The church we were attending was in the northern suburbs of Detroit, and heavily populated by auto workers and union members. Several of the elders called me out, to correct me. If the union said to strike, they explained, then they would. Their allegiance was not to their employer, but to the union.

I thought that position was inconsistent with the clear intent of the scripture, but held my thoughts, as they were elders, and I still a relatively young Christian. There must be something they knew that I didn't.

For a time, the church was without a pastor. One was hired. On his first Sunday, he introduced himself to me, thanked me for teaching the adult Sunday school class, and informed me that he would be taking it over. I had been fired from my volunteer position.

I was stunned. My class was well attended and well liked. I was gifted as a teacher, had a B. of Education and a Master of Arts in Teaching degree, and everyone seemed to love the class. I was certainly more qualified than he to lead the class. And, it seemed to me that the purpose of the church was to "equip the saints for works of service," and wasn't that exactly what I was doing?

None of that mattered, of course. The message was very clear. Now that the A team had arrived, the B team was dismissed. I was a second class Christian, and the professionals were now taking over.

This incident just clarified my understanding that in the church, there were the first class, professional Christians, like pastors and missionaries, and then there were the second class, lay people. No matter how gifted or committed I was, in the eyes of the professionals I was going to always be a second class Christian.

**No matter how gifted or committed I was,
in the eyes of the professionals,
I was always going to be a second class Christian.**

The idea that I could have a real one-to-one relationship with God, with no pastor in between, never really got traction with me. I had heard people talk about it, but it never really resonated with my experience.

Chapter Fourteen

Reflections on Second Class Christians

For much of my Christian life, I've struggled with a difficult and painful image of myself: I was a second-class Christian.

No one ever said that to me in so many words, but the practices of the Christian community made it perfectly clear. Those practices have evolved in response to a belief that permeates our Christian culture so deeply that few Christians would ever question it. Unfortunately, the result of this belief is that millions of Christians, like myself, lead lives that are far less productive than God wants. And that means that the Church's influence and impact is light years away from that which it could be.

Let's gain a little perspective.

We all have deep seated beliefs that impact our view of the world. These beliefs have formed in us over a period of many years, beginning with our childhood and continuing till now. They are often so deep within us that we are not consciously aware of them. Yet, because they define how we see the world, these deep-seated beliefs shape our attitudes, impact our emotions, shape our thoughts and determine our behaviors. For want of a better word, let's call them paradigms.

These paradigms impact everything we do and can cause individuals as well as entire groups of people to act in certain ways. For example, in Christopher Columbus's day, most of the world thought that the earth was flat. This paradigm meant that they would not sail to the horizon, because they did not want to fall off the earth. It took someone like Columbus to question that paradigm and act differently. Prior to his journey, people were held back by their beliefs - - this paradigm -- not by the reality of the situation.

The same is true for all of us. Our paradigms impact everything that we do, because they color our perceptions of what the world is really like. These deep-seated beliefs help us to make sense out of the world around us. Without them, we'd be unable to function.

However, we are always at risk of nurturing paradigms that incorrectly interpret the world and cause us act in ways that are not positive. I believe that the modern Church has been rendered ineffective by some paradigms of this nature.

I became a Christian when I was 24 years old and have walked with the Lord ever since. For much of these 30+ years, I have been puzzled by what I have seen as a mystery. On one hand, I read in the New Testament about the early church and see that it was filled with the Spirit, enthusiastic, energetic, joyful and victorious. In a very short time, it had penetrated into much of the known world. That's the church that the Lord established. But then, I look around me, and see a church that is apathetic, passive and lethargic. I look at my own life and am disappointed by the feeble expressions of the gifts of the Spirit.

This contradiction between the vibrant church of the New Testament and the apathetic church of 21st Century America has always been a source of puzzlement to me. Why, I've wondered, is that? When we have the same Spirit as the early Christians, why was the power of that Spirit so much more visible and powerful than it is today?

I've recently discovered an image that helps me to understand. Imagine this. Imagine that you have a large wooden box that is open on one side. The inside of the box is lined with shiny aluminum foil. Inside the box is a powerful light in the shape of a globe. Now imagine that you place that box in a dark room and turn on the light. It would allow a powerful beam of light to shine from the open side, illuminating everything around it.

That's sort of like us and the Holy Spirit. We're the box that contains the light, and the Holy Spirit is the light shining out from us, illuminating a dark world.

Now, take a screen, like the kind that we use on windows and doors to keep the bugs out. Nail that screen over the open side of the box. What will be the effect? The screen will have slightly cut down on the amount of light shining out of the box. The light will still be there, just as powerful as ever, but the screen will have hindered its impact on the world outside of the box. And what would happen if you would then nail layer after layer of screens on that open side of the box? With each succeeding layer, you would have hindered a little bit more of the light, until the light has been totally contained.

Our errant paradigms are like those screens nailed to the opening. We have the Holy Spirit in his full expression, just as the early Christians did, but we have hindered that expression and power of the Holy Spirit by nailing layer after layer of incorrect paradigms over the power of the Holy Spirit. Not one of them is sufficient to totally hinder the power of the Spirit, but the sum total of all of them does the job.

In this chapter, I want to try to pry one screen off by examining our paradigm concerning what we consider to be "ministry." It's this paradigm that has caused me to think of myself as a second-class Christian.

Here's the paradigm. See if it doesn't sound familiar.

Real ministry is defined by the time you spend in the official efforts of the church to evangelize the lost and edify the saved. This is the work that God is interested in, that He considers most important, special and significant.

If you are like most Christians, you are nodding your head, thinking, "Of course, who would ever question that?"

The expressions of this are all around us. Remember, paradigms shape our attitudes and determine our behavior. So, we can look at attitudes and behavior and use them to discover the paradigm that lies under the surface.

Here are some examples of this paradigm in practice. One of my clients recently indicated to me that one of his salespeople had left the company to go into the "full time ministry." We all know what he means by that. This person is going to make his living in some sanctioned work of some church. That's real ministry. What he was doing before was just making a living.

A few years ago, I read Bob Buford's book entitled, "Halftime." I was impressed with it and bought several to give to friends. The premise of the book, written primarily to Christian business people, was that now that in the first half of your life you have achieved some degree of success, use the second half to do something significant. Donate your time, money and talents to a ministry. Another expression of the paradigm.

It's not unusual to hear a pastor or fellow Christian talking about "God's work," or referring to the church building as "God's house." This kind of language indicates, of course, that God is more interested in these things then he is other things that are not "God's work" or places that are not "God's house."

I could site hundreds of other examples, but you get the idea. This concept of ministry is a deeply held, pervasive paradigm that is embraced to some degree by almost all of 21st Century Christendom.

But let's take a moment to consider the implications of this paradigm.

Consider that if some work is significant, what does that say about other work? Insignificant. If some effort is special, what does that say about other work? Ordinary. If some work is important, what does that say about other work? Unimportant.

In other words, if we hold "church work" to be special, significant and important, than this says that the rest of our lives are ordinary, insignificant and unimportant.

But is that what the Bible teaches? Hardly. In fact, it's just the opposite. For example, Paul said that everything we do, if we do it as a service to Christ, is important:

> Whatever you do, work at it with all your heart, as working for the Lord, not for men, since you know that you will receive an inheritance from the Lord as a reward. It is the Lord Christ you are serving. I Cor 3: 23, 24 (NIV)

Clearly ministry in the Bible is not determined by what is done, but rather by for whom it is done. Whatever you do for Christ is ministry.

God's work and will for this world is far greater than just those activities we know as "church work." God desires to extend the kingdom into every aspect of His creation. And he expects us to be obedient to Him and offer our lives as ministry, to extend His influence into every nock and cranny of His world. When we go to a meeting at our children's school, we are taking Christ's influence with us, extending His impact into that aspect of creation. When we go to work, we are extending Christ's influence into those contacts with people that we connect with. When we talk with a neighbor, fill the car up with gas, cut the grass, or shop for groceries, we are Christ's ambassadors, extending His influence into those realms.

Jesus called us to be the salt of the world. He intentionally chose that analogy. Salt has no value when it is held inside the salt shaker crushed against other grains of salt. It is only when it is mixed with other things that salt imparts its influence on that around us. So too for us. When we are huddled with one another in the confines of church buildings we are not fulfilling the ministry that God appointed to us. While time together is necessary for encouragement and

106

equipping, it's a means to an end. The end is our influence in our ministries that we call our lives.

Jesus called us to be the salt of the world. He intentionally chose that analogy. Salt has no value when it is held inside the salt shaker crushed against other grains of salt. It is only when it is mixed with other things that salt imparts its influence on that around us.

Here's a little self-test. Imagine yourself in two totally different mental

states. In one, you believe that your talents, experience, education and the gifts that you use in your job and your family are of little interest to God. They are just the way to fill your week. The really important things to God occur only on Sunday mornings. You understand that church work is real ministry and that our lives are something that God really doesn't care that much about. He's more interested in evangelism and edification under the auspices of a church than He is in anything we might do in our daily lives. Church work is special. And what you and I do most of our lives is ordinary. Church work is significant, and what you and I do is insignificant. And, while you desire to be active and pleasing to God, you know you cannot be because you aren't ordained, you are not a full- time minister, and you have not enough time to devote to church work.

Now that you are temporarily immersed in that mindset, ask yourself some questions. How energized are you to see your life as meaningful to God? To what degree do you feel filled with the Holy Spirit every minute of the day? How close to God do you feel? How great is your Christian influence on those around you? Record your thoughts and feelings.

Now, consider the opposite paradigm. Image yourself fully accepting and believing this:

God has selected you for a special ministry, which you alone can fulfill. You believe that God has personally and specifically equipped you with experience, talents, gifts and education to use in your job and your family. He has personally given you a ministry that is incredibly important to the growth of his kingdom and directly in the center of His will. This ministry is your work and your family. Every moment of it is empowered by the Holy Spirit, ordained by God, and overseen by Jesus Christ. He has appointed you to be his unique ambassador to take His influence into every corner of His creation touched by you. What you do on Sunday morning or in regard to the institutional church is only incidental to your main and special ministry.

Now ask yourself the same questions. How enthusiastic are you? How full of the Holy Spirit? How close to God? How excited to be using your spiritual gifts? How energized are you to see your life as meaningful to God? To what degree are you inspired to and feel filled with the Holy Spirit every minute of the day? How great is your Christian influence on those around you?

If you are like most of us, you'll quickly see that the first paradigm serves to depress the power of the Holy Spirit, to isolate you

108

under the burden of a debilitating self-image, to hinder the power of the Holy Spirit in the church. Yet, the second paradigm does just the opposite, energizing you with spiritual power and purpose. The second mindset fosters an attitude of joy, peace commitment and empowerment.

Consider the impact of these two mindsets on your Christianity. Now multiply your thoughts and feelings times the millions of Christians in the world. And imagine the impact on the universal church, and consider the impact on the growth and impact of the kingdom.

The conclusion is obvious. The cultural paradigm that holds "church work" as a higher calling than real work is an insidious, debilitating concept. It's time to do away with it. It's time to recognize that our lives, when lived for Christ, are our highest and most noble ministries. We have been selected by God and empowered by the Holy Spirit to extend the kingdom into every area of creation.

The cultural paradigm that holds "church work" as a higher calling than real work is an insidious, debilitating concept.

Chapter Fifteen

White & White (continued)

In my fourth year with White and White, I began to become a little discontent. While I enjoyed my time as a sales person for White & White, I was becoming antsy. I looked ahead and saw that the era of the 100% commissioned sales person was going to come to an end, and that my earning potential would be reduced down the road a bit.

Further, I was growing bored. I had the job mastered. I had an itch to accomplish more. So, I went to Ned and told him that I wanted to do something else. I gave him a two-year time frame. If he didn't find something else for me to do, a new challenge, within two years than I would look outside the company for another opportunity.

And so he did. The company had started a new division in Grand Rapids, and it was struggling. Dick, the company president, came to see me, and offered me the position as divisional manager. Would I be interested in moving to Grand Rapids, and taking over as general manager of this start-up division? My task would be to grow it rapidly and bring it to profitability within three years.

It looked like the opportunity I was looking for, and Coleen and I talked about it, prayed about it, and I accepted the job. A short time later we had moved the family to Grand Rapids, and I took over as General Manager for the company that was to become Accupac.

At that time, when a person was admitted to a hospital, he was generally given an "admission kit." These varied from hospital to hospital, and consisted of some inexpensive toiletries, maybe a small box of facial tissues, perhaps a disposable bed pan, maybe a laundry bag, etc. Each hospital has their own specifications, so that the kit for that hospital was put together just for it.

This ability to personalize and customize was totally outside of the competencies of the parent company, and it was felt that a separate organization could learn how to do that and extend those lessons to other similar products.

We started in the humblest of situations – a bit of rented space in the back of someone else's warehouse, with a chain link fence separating the two operations and a pre-fab office sitting on the floor of the warehouse. I had two part-time employees.

But, I had the backing of the parent company, and began to grow the business almost immediately. Over the next three years, we expanded into custom medical products of all kinds, and even moved into sterile procedure packs for specific surgeons. The move into sterile kits was a huge step, because it brought the need for a clean room to assemble the kits in, access to sterilization, and government regulation and inspection. All these were new competencies we had to discover and incorporate.

One of the greatest challenges, though, was sales! For the first couple of years, I had only the parent company's sales force. And, I had no line authority over them. I could only hope to influence them to sell my product, in the same way that an outside manufacturer would attempt to influence them to sell his product.

As time went on, I developed a sales force of several independent reps, and my own dedicated sales people. It was here that I formulated many of the concepts that would later crystalize in The Kahle Way® Sales Management System.

Over the next three years, I changed the name of the company, moved into a new building, hired about 20 people including sales people, developed all the company policies and procedures and grew the business from next to nothing to over $600,000 in monthly sales. The business grew dramatically. By the end of the third year, we were doing about $6 million dollars of annualized business, had moved twice and had a couple of dozen employees.

This was the first time that I really managed people, and it was a growing, learning time for me. It was a demanding three years, and I invested heavily in terms of time and emotional energy.

Spiritually, it was a watershed time as well. My relationship with the Lord continued on the same track that I had been on. I continued to see Christianity as primarily involved in the church, and felt I had an obligation to be as involved in the church as I could be.

In our new home in Grand Rapids, we happened onto a small, independent congregation who clearly needed us. We found ourselves at a little church in the rural areas a few miles outside of town. They were very friendly, very needy, and had a charismatic pastor, a welcoming attitude, and appeared to be growing. We became members, and almost immediately were cast into significant roles. Within just a few months, I was teaching the adult Sunday school class, and Coleen had become the congregation's crises counselor.

Within a year or so, I was asked to become one of the elders, and did so. I joined two other men in that position.

The church soon became a more significant part of our lives than ever before. I was one of three elders and we seemed to be involved in almost every work of that congregation.

At this point, I continued to see Christianity as primarily being defined by the involvement with the local church. But several events in the next couple of years began to change my perspective and shape my evolving view of the institutional church.

The first was the church split that was orchestrated by the pastor in one of the most devious, underhanded and manipulative plots I had ever experienced. Remember, at this time, I was heavily invested in the church. We attended three times a week, I taught the adult Sunday school class, served as an elder, and had a hand in almost every effort of the congregation.

The pastor was a charismatic guy who could sing, play the piano and bring an encouraging message from the pulpit.

One of the things that concerned me was the lack of written policies and procedures. It seemed that every decision was a negotiation when it didn't have to be. The three elders, and the pastor, began an effort to create some guidelines and role definitions.

As this effort moved forward, we decided to take a weekend retreat to hash out the final document. The pastor refused to join us because he had something against one of the other elders. So, the three elders went anyway.

Immediately following our retreat, we met with the pastor to discuss what we had decided upon. He showed up at the meeting at my house with another person, a brand new Christian man, and announced that the meeting had a different agenda. He was going to start a new church and was taking a third of the congregation with him. We were going to have "a family event." We could either cooperate and witness the birth of a new church, or not cooperate, and he would guarantee a nasty divorce.

I was blindsided! Where on earth did this come from? Did things like this really happen in the Lord's church? This was on Thursday evening. On Sunday, a third of the congregation was gone, as was the pastor. They just didn't show up.

I was one of two elders left. (One had gone with the pastor.) We grudgingly gave our approval (neither one of us wanted to be involved in a nasty divorce!), and then dealt with the remains.

For the next year or so, I doubled as the de-facto pastor. In addition to the Sunday school class, I brought the message from the pulpit once or twice a month and was involved in every administrative decision.

The other elder and I set about seeking the Lord's will for the congregation. We decided to use this time to investigate the organization of the church according to the scriptures, and to re-do the church on scriptural grounds.

Our Bible study lead us to a number of conclusions. First, we didn't find the role of "pastor" anywhere in the New Testament.

We didn't find the role of "pastor" anywhere in the New Testament.

The only time the word is used is in the oft-quoted passage of Ephesians 5. Interesting, the Greek word which is there translated as "pastor" appears a number of other times in the New Testament. In every other occurrence, it is translated as "shepherd" and refers to Christ, or "elder" and refers to the elders of the church. There is no defendable reason to translate it in any other way than "elder."

We came to the conclusion that the modern-day role of "pastor" was a non-biblical vestige of the traditions of the Roman Catholic Church.

The New Testament church knows nothing of the individual who is a paid, hired custodian of the congregation.

We found the roles of evangelist, elders and deacons, and decided to follow those scripture guidelines. We would not hire a pastor; we would support an evangelist.

So, we wrote up a position paper, citing those scriptures which enlightened that position, and began to look for an evangelist to

116

support. We interviewed a number of men, who all said the same thing, "Yes, this is what scripture teaches. But, it will never work." I found that statement puzzling. If it was God's work, how could it not work?

Eventually we found a man who was excited to work as an evangelist and brought him into the church in a paid position. He did not preach from the pulpit, we saw that as the responsibility of the elders, and he and his family were members of the congregation.

The next year proved the professional Christians whom we interviewed to be wrong. We brought about 100 people to salvation, (in a congregation of about 80) and almost every adult was involved in some ministry. Not only did it work, but it worked very well -- at least for a while. (For a more detailed description of this concept and our experiences, see my book, *"Is the Institutional church really the church?"*)

These years were pivotal in my business and spiritual development. Where I had been blind-sided by the pastor's manipulation, I would be blind-sided again, but in the business world.

Dick, the company president, and I went over a weekend to a national association meeting. I was nominated to be the president of the national association, but Dick said he wanted me to focus on the business and so I declined. On the plane on the way back, we discussed plans for the coming year and some of the challenges I was facing. That was Sunday afternoon.

The following Thursday, he called me up and asked me to come over and visit him. When I came into his office, he announced that he had decided to let me go. No explanation, he just "felt it was the thing to do." After eight years with the company, in which I had been the number one sales person, and build the new division from nothing to a substantial organization, I was out of a job. It was the company policy to not provide severance pay. I had two weeks' vacation pay coming. After that, I had no source of income.

It really was a shock to me. I had not seen it coming, and to this day, don't understand why it happened. There was no explanation.

But, I didn't have the luxury of wallowing in self-pity. I had a family to support, and no means of income.

I originally thought that finding a new position would not be difficult. I had a great resume and a solid record of success and contribution. I soon learned that I also had some overpowering negatives. First, my income level scared people. "You won't be happy here," I'd hear, "you will make quite a bit less than you are used to." The other negative was my experience as a divisional manager. I'd apply for sales positions, sales manager jobs, and VP's of sales. I'd always hear the same thing, "You've been a general manager, so this will be a step down. You won't last." After a number of months, I came to the conclusion that I was not going to get a job.

Since I was unable to get a new job, and I had five children and a family to support, I reasoned that I had to find a number of small jobs. And thus began my consulting practice.

Chapter Sixteen

Reflections: Best Practices for Sales People

One of the most debilitating myths about the sales profession is that sales people can learn on their own, on the job, and eventually become good at their jobs. This myth implies they'll eventually develop their own style, and that will bring them the maximum results.

That myth is true for about five percent of the sales people in the world. For the other 95 percent, nothing could be further from the truth.

The overwhelming majority of field sales people perform at a fraction of their potential because they have never been systematically exposed to the best practices of their profession. Instead, they have been expected to "learn on their own."

I like to paint. I don't mean pictures, I mean walls and bedrooms and hallways. I enjoy the physical nature of it, and the resulting change in the feeling of the room. I've always liked to paint and have done so for over 30 years. Once, for about two months, I actually made a living doing it. I think I'm pretty good at it.

Until a little while ago, when I was watching one of those reality home improvement shows. On it, a professional painter demonstrated

119

the best way to apply masking tape, hold a brush and apply the paint. Yikes! I was doing it all wrong.

All this time I thought I was pretty good, in my own self-taught, learn-on-my-own sort of way. I guess I really didn't have any standard. But I almost always painted by myself and had only my own opinion. I thought I was pretty good compared to what I thought was good.

Then, when I discovered the best practices of a true professional, I saw that my own ideas we not up to the standard. I wasn't nearly as good as I thought I was. If I'm going to become really good -- objectively, verifiably good -- I have to change my routines and incorporate the best practices.

So, it is with sales as well. The world is full of sales people who have learned on the job, pretty much on their own, and have never been exposed to the best practices of the profession. They delude themselves, as I did, holding the opinion that they are pretty good. And that delusion keeps them lingering in levels of performance considerably beneath what their potential would allow them.

Sales managers often share that delusion, and occupy themselves with other matters, unable or unsure how to improve the performance of their team. Typically, the sales manager was, in a previous incarnation, a high performing sales person. He/she was part of the five percent who learned on their own, who studied the best practices, and who incorporated them into his routines. As a result, that sales manager, formerly high performing sales person, expects every other sales person to be just like him; to have the same motivation, the same drive, the same ability and propensity to learn.

He, therefore, makes little effort to expose the sales team to best practices, because he did it on his own.

That's too bad. Every profession in the world develops a body of knowledge about the best way to do that job. And every professional in the world is expected, if they are serious about the profession, to regularly study those best practices, and to incorporate them into their routines with a disciplined, methodical effort. That's why teachers have in-services, doctors go to conferences, nurses have in-service training, etc.

The job of the sales person is no different. There is probably no other profession more written about, and to, than field sales. Over the last 50 years, there must have been thousands of books written, tens of thousands of articles published, thousands of audio programs prepared, and hundreds of newsletters and magazines published – all for the field sales person, and all describing the best practices of the profession in various terms and methods.

Just as there is a set of best ways to paint a room, so there are sets of best ways to ask a question, seek an appointment, build rapport, make a presentation, close the deal, and follow up on the purchase. Astute sales people understand this, and seek to continually expose themselves to the best practices. They continually work on incorporating the best practices into their routines, repeating them until they become habits.

Astute sales managers do likewise. They continually expose their sales people to the best practices of the profession and encourage every sales person to improve by methodically incorporating them into their routines.

Those companies that systematically and methodically expose their sales people to the body of knowledge regarding best practices of the sales profession consistently out-perform those who don't.

It is the path to improvement that the rest of the professional world understands. It's time for the sales profession to do likewise.

Chapter Seventeen

The start of the consulting practice

I discovered that I was not going get a job, and thus my only option was to find "lots of small jobs." And that was how I started the consulting practice. Building the consulting business was one of the most difficult things I have ever done. True, I had had some previous success in sales and in growing a business. But in all of those circumstances, I was part of a larger organization that provided support, capital, institutional knowledge and resources. Now, I was completely on my own. I started out with absolutely nothing. I had no contacts and virtually no local network. I had never done this before, nor did I know anyone who had successfully done it.

I never had the luxury of having a severance package. And, I had the constant pressure of having to support my family. I qualified for unemployment benefits and took full advantage of them. Coleen got a part-time job at the local grocery store. We cashed in our 401K account, and lived on the combination of those things while I tried to make a living.

I took every job or project that I unearthed. That meant telemarketing for an advertising company, raising money for a horse farm, helping hire sales people for a mortgage broker, and on and on it went. The first full year I did that, I made less money in gross revenue than I had paid in taxes the year before.

When people ask me if I was ever tempted to quit, I tell them that I did not have that option. I was convinced that I was not going to get a job, and I had a family to support. Really and truly, failure was not an option.   Plus, I was beginning to see that this was the direction that the Lord wanted me to take. I had a sense of being directed and guided by God.

One of the ways that God works with me is this. He eliminates all other options, so that I only have one choice. That is what happened over and over in building the consulting practice. Whenever I thought about some other way to make a living, He would put a road block up so that it didn't develop. For example, I would, from time to time, see a job that sounded promising. But the interviews always ended up with the prospective employer thinking I was over-qualified, or too expensive. So, back to focusing on the consulting business. It was the only option I had.

I did a SWOT analysis of what I brought to the market. I was a gifted teacher and had both a B of Ed and a M.A. in Teaching degrees. I had some excellent sales experience and had built a business from the ground floor to $6 million in sales in about three years. It occurred to me that I had learned how to grow people, grow sales territories, and grow a business. So, I called myself "The Growth Coach" and promoted myself as a consultant who could help my clients grow their sales and their people.

On the weaknesses and threats side of the equation, I had some significant obstacles. First, I had never done this before, and had to learn everything on my own. Secondly, I had almost no personal network. While I was well known in some national circles, I knew almost no one in Grand Rapids, outside of the people in our church. And, I was one of just a handful of business people there.

Third, I had no capital. On the contrary, our financial situation was such that I needed to generate income every month.

The pressure was on to figure this thing out quickly. I got all the books I could find on how to grow a consulting practice. One major suggestion was to give seminars. I knew I could speak and teach from my experience in the church and the seminars for surgeons I had done for US Surgical. So, I approached a local business college with a proposal: Let's do a joint venture series of seminars for local business people. I'll create and present the seminar, you promote it and provide the venue and the financial administration. We'll split the proceeds.

They agree, and for several years, every business owner in Grand Rapids received a brochure from the college with my picture on it, promoting some seminar I was presenting.

The practice began to grow, and the second year we actually lived off the proceeds. It would be five more years until I had equaled the income level of my previous position.

As is typically the case, I began doing almost anything for almost anyone. Anything to get some cash to pay the house payment or buy groceries.

As I read my journals from those days, I see someone who was incredibly anxious for the state of his income. It seemed like I was constantly on the verge of going under. What could I do to get enough income this month to pay the bills? What could I do to do the same next month? While I knew, intellectually, that the Lord would take care of us, I had a difficult time internalizing that emotionally and spiritually. It was a time of turmoil and doubt and constant questioning. Years later, I would look back at this and see that the Lord was preparing me for what I would do later.

I discovered that my experience with White & White had given me knowledge of sales of a set of best practices from a company that was larger and more sophisticated than my clients. I also found that the variety of different sales experiences that I had -- remember, everything from retail to capital equipment to wholesale distribution -- had given me a broader perspective on the world of sales than almost everyone else doing what I did. I had, unbeknown to me, a body of knowledge that would be valuable to my clients.

The business grew every year and the financial pressures gradually eased. After a few years, I faced a decision that I would reexamine every couple of years from then on. Should I expand the business locally, bring in other consultants, and build a company, or should I increase my fees, deepen my content and market, and stay a single person practice? For a lot of reasons, which I now see as the Lord guiding me, I always choose the latter. And, every time I confronted that decision, which I did dozens of times, I always came down on the side of building a practice, not a business.

My involvement in the local Chamber of Commerce led me into what would become an important part of my practice years later. I was on a sub-committee with two other people, and the three of us developed the concept of a CEO roundtable. This is a group of CEOs of various businesses who get together once a month, and share with each other, act as an advisory board, and support and encourage one another.

We organized the very first of these programs in the area. I wrote the curriculum for training the group facilitators, and actually trained the first couple sets of facilitators. I also developed a number of these CEO groups for the Chamber of Commerce and facilitated all the meetings. The concept proved very valuable, and the program soon became the flagship program of the Grand Rapids Area Chamber of Commerce. I saw the potential for an income stream to add to my consulting practice, and, tapping into my knowledge of wholesale distributors, formed my own private group of distributor CEOs from various industries and trade groups. They paid a monthly fee, and I organized and facilitated the meetings. One group filled up successfully, and I soon developed two private groups, as well as a couple of the free Chamber groups.

On the spiritual side, we had left the church where I had been an elder and began looking for another. Over the next couple of years, we visited dozens of churches. Sometimes we'd stay for a few months, but mostly we'd just move on. I began to feel that there was something wrong with us. Other people seemed to be happy here, or so it seemed. We just couldn't not get comfortable and committed to any church.

My disenchantment with the institutional church lead me to investigate the house church movement. My interest in church structure and organization, from a biblical perspective, had taken me to the point where I had little use for the institutional church. I added my Bible study on the subject with my personal experiences with professional Christians, and, on a good day, I considered the institutional church to be God's plan B – not what He had in mind, but He was willing to work with it. On a bad day, I considered it to be one of Satan's greatest coups.

I became convinced that the house church was the purest expression of God's intention for his people. We looked around for a house church to be involved in. Over the course of a year or so, we visited a number of house churches in the Grand Rapids area.

I became convinced that the house church was the purest expression of God's intention for his people.

Everyone was just too far away for us to attend regularly. Finally, I became convinced that the Lord wanted me to start one. This took some doing, as I was still reeling from my time as an elder, and really did not want the responsibility to oversee or organize anything. But, I realized that if we were going to be a part of a house church, I was going to have to organize it.

So we did. We found a number of like-minded people and began to meet every Sunday afternoon in one of our homes. The house church became then, for five or six years, a major part of our life. Our youngest daughter, Kelly, was raised in the house church,

128

whereas the older kids we all raised in the institutional church. I often attribute the experience as being formative in Kelly's significant spiritual development.

This was a time of serious spiritual development for all of us. The house church was so different from the formulas and programs of the institutional church. We would always have a meal together, spend quite a bit of time catching up on each other's weeks, pray for one another, have the Lord's Supper, sometimes sing together, and sometimes study the Bible together. When I was asked by skeptical ICM's (institutional church members) what we do, I would often reply, "We help one another get through life together."

I became an advocate for the house church movement. I soon discovered

a group called the open church ministry that was built around Jim Ruitz's book, The Open Church, a seminal book on the history of the institutional church and the call for reformation. Coleen and I attended a conference in St. Louis for the group and I had my first experience with a prophetic word.

At one of the prayer sessions, one of the other participants called to me and said he had a prophetic word for me. God had told him to tell me that I would write small booklets, he said, and be known as a church reformer.

I was shaken. I had never before even considered the possibility that God would want to say something specifically to me. And here He was, in a very public way, saying something to me personally.

On return to Michigan, I got involved with the ministry and became the Michigan coordinator. In that role, we organized a couple of state-wide conferences of house church people and made several trips to places around the state where there was a person or group interested in starting a house church. We would meet with them and help them in that direction.

This was a new experience for me. I found that I was actually developing a relationship with God. It was no longer about church attendance and involvement in the programs of the institutional church, God was now, at least on one occasion, communicating to me directly.

I was evolving in my Christianity to a new and more meaningful place.

It was no longer about church attendance and involvement in the programs of the institutional church, God was now, at least on one occasion, communicating to me directly.

Chapter Eighteen

South Africa

As I was struggling to make a living as a consultant, the Lord began to work on us in other ways.

We were becoming interested in being missionaries to South Africa. It appeared more and more likely that the Lord was leading us in that path. We began to correspond with missionaries in South Africa and went around to churches who invited us to bring a sermon from the pulpit and ask for support.

We had accumulated a sum of money that churches had given to us as a result of our effort to acquire support, but none had committed to on-going support. We were definitely at a road block.

So, we decided to use the money to take a short-term trip to South Africa, and see if that wouldn't shake things loose, and provide us with some clarity. This was in the days of apartheid, and South Africa was seen as a very dangerous place. We had corresponded with American missionaries and felt certain we would be safe. So, we sent the older kids to stay with friends, packed our six-year old with us, and headed out for six weeks in South Africa.

We flew into Johannesburg, rented a car, and set out on a six-week tour of the country, moving from one missionary with whom we had corresponded to another.

What an eye-opener. We traveled from one end of the country to the other, spending a few days with each of the missionaries with whom we had corresponded. And we discovered something that blew away our previous notions. Most of the missionaries we visited didn't really do very much. They had homes with swimming pools, maids and gardeners, but many probably didn't spent more than eight hours a week in "missionary work." In the car driving away from the missionary's home, Coleen and I would talk about each visit, and I found myself asking time and time again, "What do they do all day?"

Here is an example. One missionary had been there for most of his life. He sent monthly newsletters home to his supporters, with pictures of him teaching a Sunday school class. However, teaching that Sunday school was the only thing he did. That's what we would expect of any Christian, not someone who was being supported full-time.

Another took us with him to visit a congregation, where I brought the sermon. We overheard the missionary speaking with one of the congregation's leaders, who mentioned that he hadn't seen the missionary for over two years.

We probably visited a dozen missionaries. We found two, one in Johannesburg, and one in Cape Town, that appeared to be truly committed, and working full time in the work of the Lord. The missionary in Johannesburg had a large home in the downtrodden area of Johannesburg and ran a ministry out of it to the poor. The missionary in Cape Town also was active in educating and supporting the local indigenous churches.

We left South Africa convinced that, while most of the American missionaries seemed to have found the gravy train – an easy life with little real responsibilities – that there were huge opportunities to work with the native Christians, who were hungry to learn. We felt that we could fit into the culture and be effective. The rest were, at the best, lazy, and at the worst, deceptive malingerers.

We developed a special affinity for Steve Zimmerman in Cape Town and fell in love with the city and its people. Steve assured us that we could be effective on a regular part-time basis and promised to work with us if we chose to do that.

We came back with the clarity we had hoped to find. While we were not going to be full-time missionaries, we could do the work on a regular part-time basis.

We experienced what so many travelers to Africa have remarked on. There is something incredibly alluring about Africa. It is almost a spiritual thing. You just feel this intense attraction to the land.

We found the varieties of tribes and the entire tribal culture to be interesting. The apartheid separation of the races based on the skin color was hard to understand. We discovered a phenomenon which were later to see almost every in the world we traveled. If you are an American business person, you are immediately credited with being wise and knowledgeable. People attribute immediate credibility to you. This became one of our primary strengths in the work that we later did as short-term missionaries.

Once we had resolved the issue of being full time missionaries in favor of being regular part-time missionaries, I began to get serious about building a consulting business. I actually had business cards printed and began to work at creating some customers. The first couple of years were a tremendous struggle. And, in that year following my last with Accupac, I made less than I had paid in taxes the previous year.

God was at work in our lives in other ways as well. While we had such a positive experience at the church, it wasn't to last. Coleen and I began to burn out from the intensity of our involvement, – I was still teaching the adult class, bringing the message from the pulpit once a month, building the business, and, Coleen and I were raising four of our own children, plus a succession of foster children.

We had gone to on our first mission trip to South Africa and realized that we are probably never going to be full time missionaries. However, we had some money that had been given to us for the purpose, we had created some relationships with key people in South Africa, and we were convinced that we could be effective as regular short-term missionaries.

At the same time, the old guard at the church continued to lobby for a "leader." We decided it was time to step down and out and did so. The congregation made the evangelist into a traditional pastor, the church stopped growing, and everyone eased into their comfortable pre-Dave routines A few years later, it split again.

Over the next ten years or so, we went back to South Africa on month-long mission trips about ten times, staying in Cape Town each time and working under the direction of our American missionary friend there.

At this point, I thought that the church split orchestrated by the former pastor was one of the most deceptive and evil things I could imagine in the church. But it was nothing compared to what happened next. The Lord used a set of experiences to draw me closer to my understanding of the 'business as mission' concept, and to begin to formalize my view of the institutional church.

Here's how He did it. Our experience on our first trip to South Africa has convinced us that we had great credibility as an American business person who was interested in helping people grow spiritually. We also saw that there was, alongside the native African culture, a 21st century modern economy in which cellphones, computers, sky scrapers and freeways were all a part.

So, we determined to try to help fund our trips by trying to line up some speaking engagements or consulting projects while we were there. We were successful in aligning with a couple of seminar promoting companies, and on several of the trips, I was able to help defer our costs by presenting sales and sales management seminars.

At the beginning of this time, we were moving away from my involvement in the local congregation. I had stepped down as an elder. However, the elders of that congregation were the official custodians of the funds we had accumulated during our attempts to find supporters. We were uncomfortable with that and looked around for some other arrangement. We discovered what seemed like a match made in heaven. In Lansing, just 50 miles away, was the headquarters of a small mission effort that, among other things supported one of the American missionaries in Cape Town. While we had met him in South Africa, we had never spent any time with him, and didn't really know him.

We approached the directors of that mission effort and described our situation – that we intended to do regular short-term mission trips to Cape Town, that we expected to fund them ourselves, and that we felt we needed the legitimacy of being associated with an existing mission effort.

In addition, we had this small amount of money that had been given to us for this purpose and wanted to move it from the oversight of our local elders to that of a mission organization. Would they be willing to have us move under their umbrella? After some deliberation on their part, they agreed.

We talked to the director of that ministry several times, explaining our situation in detail. They agreed to take oversight. The elders of our local congregation were sympathetic to our plans. We thought it best to arrange a meeting between the elders of the church, and the director of the ministry. Then, we would transfer the funds to the non-profit, and go from there.

The elders arrived at our home first. Shortly thereafter, the two folks from Lansing showed up. After introductions were made, the professional Christians from Lansing announced that they had no intention of taking oversight of our work or money. They further proclaimed that they thought mixing business with ministry was not possible and was sinful. They were suspicious that I wanted to use the mission funds to further my business interests and would have no part in it. I was a charlatan, in their opinion, an evil business person and not to be trusted. They left.

Incredible! Not only had they lied to us about their intentions, but they plotted to make a dramatic statement. They could have taken that position over the phone, but instead opted for this theatrical event. Once again, I was shocked and disillusioned by the deceitful, immoral behavior on the part of these "professional" Christians.

To this day, I'm not sure what their motivation was. While the missionaries could have just refused to work with us, instead they chose this dramatic, almost theatrical presentation. Perhaps they wanted to try to prevent our coming back to Cape Town. Or maybe they just couldn't get their heads around the idea that you could be both a business person and a missionary.

Regardless, I was floored. The local elders were shocked as well. But they knew us and knew the missionaries' accusations to be false.

In my view, something was clearly wrong. At the same time, I saw that problem as the church, not the Savior.

The problem was the church, not the Savior.

My wife and I took several short-term mission trips to South Africa. The consulting practice afforded us the income and flexibility to

137

do this. We were, for the most part, self-funded and independent. We maintained our connections with South Africa, and eventually made ten additional short-term mission trips to work with Steve in Cape Town.

Chapter Nineteen

Big lesson learned: The professionals who run the church cannot be counted on to act like Christians.

My experience with Christian Dynamics put a damper on my new-Christian enthusiasm and provided me with the first in what was to become a long list of disappointments and disillusionments with the institutional church.

As a new Christian, I was full of enthusiasm for the Lord and wanted to be as pleasing to Him as I could be. I knew I had talents and gifts, and I felt a stewardship responsibility to use them. At that time, I was still firmly caught up in the paradigm that the way to grow as a Christian was through involvement in the church.

I saw Christian Dynamics and the partnership with the big-name preacher to be the perfect place for me to use my talents to foster the Lord's church. His cowardly disappearance really shook me.

It seemed like the church was a dangerous place for a Christian.

Over the next decade, the Lord continued to teach me this lesson, over and over again. There was the dismissal from my role as

139

Bible school teacher by the pastor intent on solidifying his position, the power-hungry pastor who split the congregation where I was an elder, the lazy missionaries in South Africa, and finally the malevolent mission directors who visited our home in an attempt to humiliate us.

It took a while, and a continuous stream of disappointments, for me to realize that the institutional church just wasn't where the Lord wanted me. There were just too many professional Christians who didn't act like Christians.

My views of the church were now being radically transformed. I was done with the institutional church. Time after time I was lied to and manipulated by people who were supposed to be the paragons of Christianity. I was disillusioned, to say the least. My conclusion formed a big lesson: You can't count on the professionals who ran the church to act like Christians.

Chapter Twenty

Expanding to a national practice

The consulting business began to grow. Just as importantly, I began to recognize certain things in me that I had not be aware of before. For example, I began to realize that I had gained knowledge of sales and sales management that was broader and deeper than that which resided in my clients. I discovered that I had a gift of being able to assess a situation in my clients and almost immediately cut to the heart of the matter and create a solution. I discovered that I had the ability to create learning content that other business people found valuable and were willing to invest time and money into. I discovered that I had a natural ability to present, in both large and small groups.

Prior to these first few years in the consulting practice, I was totally unaware of those gifts and abilities. I had a sense that the Lord was guiding my path. As I struggled to define my practice and a market, I became sensitive to doors closing and others opening on my journey. I began to see my experience, from my early days at Jewel Tea, to now actually presenting sales and sales management concepts to groups of business people, as having been orchestrated by God to give me a set of experiences, a body of knowledge, and a growing wisdom.

The business grew every year, and I grew in my confidence and the gifts and abilities that arose out of it. At one of the seminars, one of the attendees approached me at the end, remarked that the seminar was great, and asked what I would charge to present it to his company. It caught me off guard. The idea of actually speaking for a fee had never occurred to me. I saw the seminars as purely a means of feeding the consulting practice, not as a money maker by itself.

I quickly came up with a number, which I was later to learn was a fraction of what it should be and booked my first paid speaking engagement. Another door was opening. I began to expand the consulting business to now offer training as well and discovered that it was much more lucrative than the hourly rate consulting work.

The business was growing nicely, and our financial situation gradually improved. Earlier, we had cashed in our 401-K account and lived on the proceeds while I was attempting to develop the practice. Now, generally speaking, our monthly income needs were being met, and we were generating enough income to afford the mission trips to South Africa.

But there were some other issues working on me. Coleen had never liked Grand Rapids, and indicated, on several occasions that she did not want to spend the rest of her life there. If I built a consulting business in Grand Rapids, we would never be able to leave. I shifted my focus to a national market. My clients were mostly smaller companies, and I often had trouble collecting from them. I spent a good deal of time attempting to collect on a receivable. And, I had the concept, lurking in my subconscious, that the Lord had something else in mind for me.

As I worked with my clients, I uncovered a common need: Very few of them had any success hiring a sales person. So, I put together one of my first "bodies of content," – a seminar entitled "How to Find, Interview, Select and Hire a Good Salesperson." The program was very well received, and eventually morphed into an audio-tape program by the same title. I began to sell these via direct mail to companies around the country (this was pre-internet days).

My first national speaking engagement

I decided that would be the content for my first full-day seminar; "How to Find, Interview, Select and Hire a Good Salesperson." I put the content together and offered it through the college. The program was very well received and seemed to provide a valuable solution to the folks who attended. I began to offer it every few months. The success of that program led me to create what was to be my first multi-media course. I recorded the program as a series of audio lessons with a printed hard-copy manual to go along with it.

We began to sell it nationally. One of the people who bought it, and appreciated it, was another trainer who happened to be dating an association executive. She told him about the program, and he made the trip to Grand Rapids from Toronto to see my presentation. On the basis of that, we came to an agreement on my first national association speaking engagement. Coleen and I flew to Toronto, and I presented an abbreviated version to the national meeting of an association of Canadian beauty-supply distributors.

The program went well, and I discovered a new source of income. I could speak at national conventions! I made more in that one day that I would have in a normal week of consulting. Plus, if I built a national speaking practice, I could live anywhere.

I joined the National Speaker's Association, went to the national convention, and began to enter into the world of professional speaking. It became clear to me that this was a specialized business, and I was a neophyte in it. I decided to hire a consultant to help me enter this world. I had a met a couple of them at the NSA convention, and decided to hire a lady in Dallas, Texas, who was a consultant to the legendary Zig Ziglar.

Off I went to Dallas, to spend a week, and have her do her magic with me. In the middle of the first morning, as I was showing her the materials from some of the seminars I had done for Davenport, she stopped me. "Do you know what you do?" she asked.

"Sure," I replied, "I do all this sales stuff."

"NO, you don't" she said. "You teach people how to think."

"I don't think so," I replied. "Look, my expertise is in sales and sales systems."

"I have a gift of being able to work with a speaker and discern their core message," she said. "Trust me, you teach people how to think. That is your message."

"I don't think so." I again replied.

"Here's what we are going to do," she said. "I am going to stop this session right now. I want you to go back to the hotel, have lunch, and then sit down and think about how you think. Write it down and bring it back. I think you will discover that you have a system."

I grudgingly agreed. Sitting in my hotel room with a yellow pad, I thought to myself, "Think about how I think! How do I even begin?"

By 7 PM that night, I had discovered a 12-step process with six overlays in a matrix. Amazing. I did have a system.

The next morning, I took that back and apologized. "You were right. Look."

"That is far too complex to teach," she said, "So you must simplify it."

With that decided we worked the rest of the week on creating some presentations and developing a marketing package. I called the system "One Step Beyond – how to think your way from chaos to positive action."

I came back to Grand Rapids more excited and focused than I had ever been. Not only did I have a game plan to build a national speaking practice, but I had a message that was powerful, unique and that could help literally millions of people.

I created a book proposal and sent it off to several agents.

Then, I decided to kick it off with a big bang. I created a half-day seminar, and organized an event to unfold that great content. I invited 50 of my clients to attend. Not only would they get the seminar for free, but I would buy them lunch at the same time. On their side, they had to bring one other person, and agree to do an in-depth evaluation.

At the seminar, I had 100 people – 50 prospects whom I had never met, and 50 clients. The seminar went well, the evaluations were glowing, and I ended the day having created some buzz and acquired a list of 100 solid prospects, who had already been exposed to the content.

I was off and running.

Or so I thought. Alas, it was not to be. Over the next couple of months, I methodically called on every one of those 100 prospects. And I did not sell one program. Not even a nibble. While they appreciated the power of the system that I taught them, they used someone else's decision-making program, or they just didn't' see the application for their employees. Every single one of them said, "The program was great, but it's not for us because.........................."

I came to the conclusion that while I had a system that could make a difference in people's lives and businesses, no one really wanted it. The overwhelming majority of people didn't want to learn to think better, they wanted someone to think for them.

I came to the conclusion that while I had a system that could make a difference in people's lives and businesses, no one really wanted it. The overwhelming majority of people didn't want to learn to think better, they wanted someone to think for them.

I wasn't able to find an agent to take the book. So, I decided to put the whole thing on the back burner and concentrate on my sales content. Over the years, I would, from time to time, resurrect the content and try to push it forward. I discovered someone else owned the trademark, One Step Beyond, and wouldn't part with it. So, I changed the name to Menta-Morphosis®, and trademarked that. I would dust it off and do a seminar every now and then. The seminars were always sparsely attended but got rave reviews.

On a couple of occasions, I hired marketing people to look at the content and develop a plan to market it. None of these were successful. To this day, the Menta-Morphosis ® content continues to take up a couple of drawers in my file cabinet and provide the greatest single disappointment of my professional life – alas, the unique message that I was born to bring has no market.

To this day, the failure of this content is my biggest professional regret. I have concepts and tools that, in some cases, are absolutely ground-breaking, but no one is interested.

I returned to my consulting practice and began to develop the things I had learned into content for sales people and sales managers. I still had aspirations to develop a national speaking practice. One of the things I learned was the power of focusing on a niche. As I looked around at my clients, my experience, and my strengths, I decided that wholesale distributors were going to be my niche. I had great experience with White & White, and a number of my clients were distributors. I looked at the industry and saw that there was no one who was visible as a sales guru for distributors.

I decided to be that. So, I wrote my first book, *How to Excel at Distributor Sales*, self-published it, marketed it nationally, and began to claim the title of the guru of distributor sales.

Slowly I began to gain visibility and credibility in that world. It was big enough to provide a market base for me, and I had content that had proven to solve common problems and provide tools for the average sales person to excel. I discovered that my teaching experience and education gave me insights into how to organize a seminar or training event to make it much more effective than the average. I also discovered a natural gift for writing.

I began to be invited to speak at conventions and national sales meetings of larger companies.

The only negative about the market is one that I've had to deal with since the beginning: Wholesales distributors are notorious penny-pinchers. As a general rule, they do not believe in spending money to educate or develop their people.

But the market was large enough to support me, even if ninety percent of the companies didn't believe in developing their people, the ten percent who did were the market leaders and they provided a large enough market.

From about 1994 to 2001, the business continued to grow. I discovered my gift for writing. I began writing articles on sales and sales management, and we evolved a system for simultaneously submitting them to hundreds of trade publications. We would keep track of how often they were published, and finally gave up on keeping track when we had recorded over 1,000.

I developed our weekly E-zine, "*Thinking about Sales.*" We created a format for the articles on sales and sales management and emailed this every week to an opt-in subscriber base that topped 40,000 in 2008.

I found it easy to write and produced eight books that found national and international markets.

I added staff, expanded the website, created products, wrote articles, added the E-zine, and found myself traveling extensively. Life was busy, but good.

Then, 9/11 hit and we experienced the same thing every other business in this country experienced – a sudden drop in activity.

Everything cancelled. Speaking engagements, consulting contracts – everything. One national convention for which I was scheduled to speak cancelled the entire convention. Our cash flow withered.

I told my staff that November 15 was the last pay day I could make. If something didn't change, we would be out of cash by then. Looking back on it, I see that in many ways we were blessed to have a fiscally conservative mind set, driven by Biblical principles of money management, that we could go seven weeks without any income and still pay everyone. If you recall, the airlines could not go four days.

At that point, we had virtually no revenue, and nothing booked. The entire country was still reeling, and no one wanted to travel, or invest in the future. I don't want to let everyone go. I decided I needed to do something – sales people still needed training in how to do their jobs better, and somebody had to take a lead in that. So, we brainstormed. People still needed training, I reasoned, they just were not interested in travelling to get it. At this time, telephone seminars (the precursor to video enhanced webinars) were beginning to gain traction. I had done a number of them and felt comfortable with the medium. I knew we could use it to deliver sales training.

So, I created a format for a one-hour sales training seminar. Download a pdf file, print the handouts, disseminate them to your sales team, and gather everyone around a speaker phone for 60 minutes on a Friday afternoon. I developed about a dozen topics, and we created an efficient system to take reservations. When phone seminars were going for $200 each, we decided to sell them for $79 each.

We decided to call them "virtual seminars," and promoted the first of them to my clients and prospects. We sold about 75 seats to the first one, and we were off and running.

For the next eight years, I did one telephone seminar every month - 84 in all. We trained, inspirited and educated thousands of sales people around the world. I changed the name to TGIF&K (Thanks Goodness it's Friday and Kahle). We went to the national associations who had hired me as a convention speaker, and offered them a discount to their members in exchange for them promoting it to their membership.

In its heyday, we had dozens of national associations sponsoring them, and I had one full time staff person who job it was to liaison with them.

We took surveys and learned that the average site had seven sales people. Using that as a measurement, we estimated that as many as 1500 sales people listened in every month. We had found the product that was to energize the business for the next few years.

Next came the Top Gun seminars. Flush with the success of the phone seminars, I decided to try live, open-enrollment sales seminars. The TGIF&K telephone seminars uncovered the need for training that was focused, practical and economical. I decided to try a live, open-enrollment seminar for sales people, implementing the same principles.

This was a big risk, because you needed to assume almost all the costs – meeting rooms, promotion, air plane tickets, etc., before you had one penny in income. Still, we felt the Lord was leading us in that direction, and so we took the risk. We had the relationships with the national associations and felt we could expand those relationships to extend to the live seminar. So, we went to our national association sponsors, and offered them the same deal – promote it to your members, and you can offer them a discount. I created a one-day interactive program for sales people, incorporating many of the principles, processes and practices from my books and private training programs. We branded it "Top Gun Sales System" and took a big risk by scheduling four seminars at strategic locations around the country.

The program was a hit, and over the next ten years, we did as many as 15 Top Gun seminars a year, all over the continent. The publicity surrounding them uncovered companies who wanted to do private programs, and often provided more income from the private programs then from the seminars themselves.

Typically, a company would send a couple of sales people to one of the programs. They would return saying good things about it, and then the company would contact me to do a private program.

In the process, I picked up two major relationships with Fortune 500 companies. My calendar was full, and during one stretch in 2008, I did speaking engagements in 23 cities on one 42-day trip.

At the same time, I continued to write books, and expand the weekly E-zine. The business continued to grow, and reached its peak in 2008, when we billed almost $1 million dollars in revenue.

Chapter Twenty-One

Big lesson learned: Your business/job is your ministry

Over this time, the Lord continued to put situations into my life that caused me to question the institutional church. At the same time, he was building something in me to take its place.

I got curious about the concept of 'ministry' and did a deep bible study on the concept. I wanted to investigate the notion put forward by the Institutional church that 'real ministry was full time work in the church.' Everything else was second class.

My study did not reveal any such thing. In fact, just the opposite. There is no standard definition of what a minister is. The word is not defined by what you do, but rather by who you serve. All work done in the name of Christ and for His glory is ministry.

Colossians 2:22-24

"Slaves, obey your earthly masters in everything; and do it, not only when their eye is on you and to win their favor, but with sincerity of heart and reverence for the Lord. Whatever you do, work at it with all your heart, as working for the Lord, not for men, since you know that you will receive an inheritance from the Lord as a reward. It is the Lord Christ you are serving. "

**Ministry is not defined by what you do,
but rather by who you serve.**

I began to read the books which began to come out on the 'business as mission' movement – a movement to recognize the anointing of business as an important area of ministry. Books like *God @ Work*, by Rich Marshall, *Your Work Matters to God*, by Sherman and Hendricks, *God Owns My Business*, by Stanley Tam, were just a few of the 'business as mission' movement books that had an impact on me. I came to the scriptures with a new perspective and noticed that almost every major work of God began with a workplace minister, not a professional Christian. Let's consider them:

Abraham. As God moved to set aside a chosen people for His covenant, he chose a wealthy farmer/rancher to do the work.

Joseph. Moving God's fledging people to Egypt so that they could multiply, it was Joseph, a business person who ran the pharaoh's food distribution system, whom God picked to facilitate this critical movement.

Moses. Royally-raised and educated, but a shepherd by vocation, Moses lead the Israelites to the Promised Land.

Nehemiah: After the captivity, God chose an executive in the King's court to supervise the re-building of the city and the organization of God's people as they reestablished themselves.

<u>Jesus:</u> A carpenter who made his living in the marketplace, he probably was a small business owner, making furniture and maybe homes for people, prior to the full-time pursuit of his ministry.

<u>Paul:</u> A life-time craftsman, he was a tentmaker, probably in sole-proprietorship, who supported himself and much of his travels in the marketplace.

The Lord unfolded all of this to me, one step at a time, until I arrived at a clear understanding: My career as a sales person, and now my business as a sales authority, was a ministry given to me by God.

I was a market place minister.

I realized that I was a market place minister!

My job was to bring God's providence and presence into every nook and cranny of the world into which my practice took me. Over the years I had gone through progression, from thinking that God was only in church, and not really interested in my job, to finding him interested and involved, to asking Him to help with my job, to asking Him to be a partner in my business, to realizing that it's His business, and asking him to show me how to be a better steward and minister of His business. From one extreme position on the spectrum to the other.

In 1998, I wrote the following mission, vision and value statement for the business, and actively tried to comply with it.

The DaCo Corporation

Vision

To continually increase our positive impact on people and organizations while remaining in the center of God's direction and reflecting His character.

Mission

To help people grow their organizations, their sales, their people, and themselves. We do this through the application of our abilities to provide consulting services, create educational products, create and deliver presentations, and provide training.

Values

Profit: We will earn a better than average profit as this allows us the flexibility to do other things.

Integrity: We will be honest in everything we do, never over promise, and zealously work to fulfill our commitments.

Value: We will strive to provide our clients more value than they expect.

Personable: We will be pleasant and easy to work with.

Knowledgeable: Understanding that we are in the business of "selling knowledge," we will be on the cutting edge of new knowledge.

Open-minded: We will constantly be open to new or different ideas, methods and concepts from all sources, especially our clients.

Learning: We will value individual and organizational learning (the ability to continually take in new information, acquire new insights, and change in positive ways as a result of that information) as our primary competitive advantage.

Humility: We will constantly be aware that the resources we use and the clients we serve are gifts from God, entrusted to our temporary stewardship.

Quality: In everything we do, we will strive to do it as well as, or better than, the very best companies in the world like ours do it.

Chapter Twenty-Two

God communicates to me

In this time of rapid growth of the business, God was working on me and with me in a number of ways. Since I was traveling so much, our house church faded away. Everyone looked on me to lead it, and when I wasn't there, no one would step in to replace me. Gradually it dispersed. While we missed it, we recognized the good things that we had gotten from it. Our youngest daughter, Kelly, was raised in the house church, as opposed to her older siblings who were subjected to the traditional institutional church environment. I attribute her mature spirituality to that.

I began to see how God was involved in the business. The decisions to specialize in distribution, to seek a national market, to do the phone seminars and then to step out and take the risk of the Top Gun seminars were all, I believe, prompted by the Holy Spirit.

One of the issues that I have confronted in my Christian life is that of hearing God's voice. It seems I regularly run into people who say "God told me to...." That always puzzled me a bit, because I had never heard God speak to me. Were they being a little too liberal with their interpretation of what constitutes God speaking, or was it me?

So, I did a major Bible search, trying to determine how God speaks to people. My conclusion was: Anyway He wants to. There is really no pattern. He has used a burning bush, a talking donkey, hand writing on the wall, His son, angels, just to name a few.

I had seen God's hand in my life, but almost always evident to me through circumstances. For example, on several occasions, the circumstances were arranged in such a way as to lead me down a certain path. Going to work for White & White, morphing into the consulting practice were just a couple of a long list of occasions when, in retrospect, I saw God arranging circumstances to guide in one path or another.

On a number of occasions, other people have said things to me that were just exactly the message I needed to hear. I often thought that maybe that was God speaking to me.

On another couple of occasions, I had a sense of complete and deep peace about an issue. Typically, this was an issue which was of great concern to me, and a subject of passionate prayer. I felt that was God communicated to me that my prayer had been answered.

However, none of these were in the class of communication that I would confidently say, "God told me to…"

That began to change when we got involved in the house church movement. I began to have communications from God in ways that I had never experienced. At a house church conference in St. Louis, during an intense prayer time, one of the folks in the group spoke up. He had a prophetic word from God for me, he proclaimed. Then, he proceeded to tell me that God had told him to tell me that I would write books, specifically small books, and be known as a church reformer. I was dumbfounded. God would say something specifically to me! Incredible. I broke into tears.

That was my first real experience where someone claimed, or I could claim, that God said this to you, outside of the scriptures – personal revelation.

Next was at a DeColores retreat. That is a non-denominational four-day retreat that is held by local groups around the world. At several times during the retreat, we were given a time of quiet reflection and prayer. During that time, two words sort of developed in my mind, sort of oozing up out of some deeper layer within me. The words were "Pride and Grace." I knew instinctively and without a doubt that they were words from God. A message for me. I didn't hear them so much as I recognized them forming in my mind and coming from a source outside of me.

I had two dreams. On both occasions, I woke up remembering the details of the dream (very unusual for me), knowing that they were from God, and knowing what the message in the dream was.

We lost our oldest daughter when she was 34 years old. It was, of course, a tremendous trauma for everyone. When she was a teenage, she committed her life to Christ, and I baptized her.

As a young adult, she had made some poor decisions in her life, and often found herself in circumstances that were less than what we would want for her.

Sometime in the weeks following her death, the Lord gave me a vision. I can't describe it. It seemed to be a glimpse into something other worldly. Maybe it lasted a fraction of a second, maybe longer. But, in the vision, I saw clearly that she was with Him, and I saw clearly how that came to be. That He loved her so much, that He would not depart from her. No matter what decisions she had made, or circumstances she had gotten herself into, His love pulled her to Him. I didn't hear it, I saw it. I just don't have words to describe the experience. But, it was clearly an individual message from God to me.

This was a vault to a new level of spiritual maturity for me. Whereas before I always saw my Christianity through the lens of the church. Now, I began to understand what it meant to have a relationship with God. A one-to-one relationship that had nothing to do with my role in the church. Whereas before I would pray to Him, and ask for His intervention in my life, for his guidance in the decisions I had to make, I was always looking for his answers to be in the circumstances of my life. It never occurred to me that He would or could speak directly to me.

Now, I began to be sensitive to the possibilities that He would communicate directly with me and began to expect direction from Him.

Chapter Twenty Three:

The next transition

The recession of 2008 had a huge impact on my business. I had some national contracts which sustained us in 2009 and the first part of 2010, but by 2010 the business was heading dramatically lower. The national contracts decided to move the work inside their organizations, and we cancelled a couple of seminars for lack of registrations. The private training programs nosedived, and we saw an 80% reduction in business.

Earlier in 2010, I saw the coming downturn coming, and with it a change in the way people thought of training. I decided to build an on-line portal. For the next year, we methodically built The Sales Resource Center®, eventually adding over 400 audio and video training programs, exams, quizzes and behavioral assessments.

Revenue was smaller than we had anticipated, and by the early spring of 2012, we found ourselves, just like at 9/11, in a place where we were scrambling to make payroll. In 2011, discretionary dollars had shriveled up almost completely, and we cancelled 10 of 11 Top Gun Seminars for lack of registrations. I downsized my staff and moved into smaller and less expensive offices. By the end of 2011, we had cut costs significantly, and reduced staff and capabilities.

In the spring of 2010 when we were seeing the business fall apart around us, I contracted with Charles and Elizabeth Robinson of Wise Ministries. They are corporate intercessors, who pray, contractually, for companies. I had had corporate intercessors in the past, but nothing as formal as this.

I would email them a prayer list every Monday morning and one of their intercessors would pray on my behalf. They would transcribe their prayer into a document and email it back. From time to time, the intercessor would also record any prophetic word that he/she felt they may have received pertaining to me and the business.

Then, once a month, I would have an hour conference with Charles, and we would basically do the same thing. In October, 2011, I was scheduled to be in Dallas to do a seminar. The Robinsons invited me to visit them in Austin, where they are located. I did. We spent the better part of a day together including a time of intense prayer. During this time when Charles and I were praying, Elizabeth was quietly drawing something on a piece of blank paper.

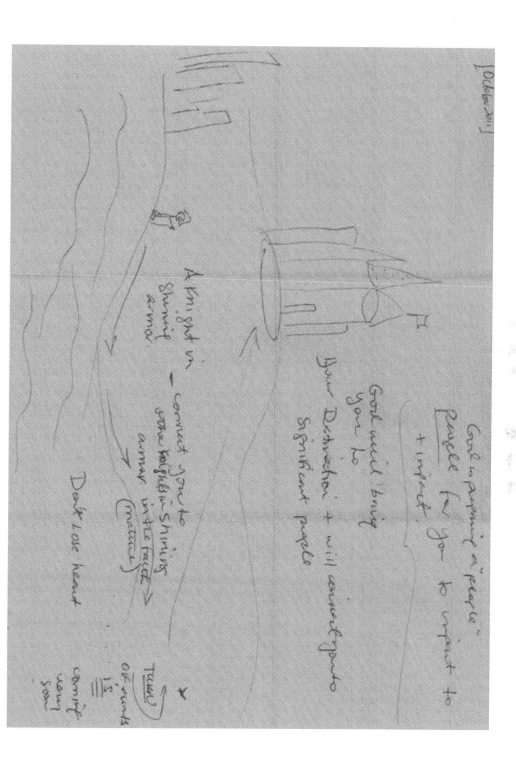

That drawing is attached. Note that she dated it October, 2011 in the upper left corner.

The drawing is of a city on the lower left, with a road leading out of it. On the road is stick figure of a "knight" in armor. The road extends to the end of the page, then turns 180 degrees and heads back to a different city in the upper left of the page.

These are the words written on the page: Next to the stick figure are the words: "A knight in shining armor." Then "Connect you other knights in shining armor in the faith (mature). Don't lose heart."

By the sharp 180-degree turn in the road are these words "turn of events is coming very soon."

Above the road leading to the new city: "God is preparing a "people" for you to impart to and impact. God will bring you to your destination and will connect you with significant people."

After the prayer time, Elizabeth shared the drawing with me, saying that it was a word from God that she received for me. She basically shared the words on the paper with me.

I didn't see anything actionable in it. There was no call for me to do anything. So, I took it with me, put it in my desk drawer and pretty much forgot it.

During this time (late winter of 2012) Charles indicated that he felt God did not want me to do anything drastic about the business until June.

As perspective, the business was hitting bottom. We went from July, 2011 through December, 2012 without a single inquiry for a speaking engagement or training session, when previously we would expect one or two a week. Just a year or two earlier, we had a million-dollar practice, with seven employees and an ongoing system to generate multiple revenue streams.

I was alternating between frustration and depression, fighting to keep my faith in that the Lord was working, when it looked like all around me things were crumbling.

I terminated the contract with Wise in February, because I could no longer afford them, and was cutting all the expenses I could. I kept in mind the idea of doing nothing radical till June and put aside several "radical" decisions like laying off my staff and moving what I was left of the business into our basement.

During the spring, I determined that we had to do something to resurrect the business. Since the public seminars had been the vehicle on which we had built the business, and since it seemed like the economy was beginning to improve, I determined to expand our seminar offerings and aggressively promote them.

So, we did a more thorough job of identifying key cities, putting together an aggressive seminar program, contracting with nine national associations to co-sponsor them, and created a more aggressive marketing program. For example, we had never previously done pay per click advertising for the seminars, but this time we did that. We had never used purchased email lists and we did that. We even dropped the price by 30%.

In 2008, we had approximately 800 people come through these seminars. This time, in the first six programs, we had one paid registration!

It occurred to me that we couldn't be that bad. This had to be supernatural. The Lord was putting an end to the public seminars, which had been the heart of the business. Our business, as we had known it, was done.

We couldn't be that bad. This had to be supernatural. The Lord was putting an end to the public sales seminars. The business, as we had known it, was done!

I did a lot of praying about it and decided that I needed to find something else to do to complement what remained of the training/consulting business. My initial instinct was to look at CEO roundtables. I had been very active in local CEO roundtables at the beginning of my practice, had managed a couple private groups, had trained all the facilitators for the Grand Rapids Chamber of Commerce CEO Roundtable program, and had even written the curriculum to train facilitators. I considered myself to be an expert facilitator.

So, I researched a number of them on-line, and identified four Christian roundtable organizations. I pursued each and eventually found myself coming to Indianapolis to sit in on a training for the Chapter Presidents of Truth@Work on June 6th.

Following the meeting, I determined that they were the group with which I wanted to associate. Shortly thereafter, I found Elizabeth's drawing in my drawer. It dawned on me that the disaster in the seminars was the sudden turn of events, and the Chapter Presidents and staff at Truth@Work were the other mature "knights in shining armor," and that the CEOs in groups I would lead were the significant people.

And, it was June. The prophecy had come true.

Chapter Twenty-Four:

Big lesson learned: God really is interested in me, and will guide, direct and speak to me.

The subject of this book has been my life outside of my home and family. In that arena, I have had discovered two themes that defined that part of my life: the ups and downs of my career and how it related to my spirituality; and my growing dissatisfaction with the institutional church, and how that related to my spirituality.

They say that life is lived looking forward and understood looking backward. If you will indulge me a bit of reflection, at this point in my life it is clear to me that God has orchestrated events and circumstances in both spheres to bring me to a point where I am today, and potentially move me to another place where He wants me.

In my career, I think back to my earliest recognition of one of my gifts – the ability to write. As a 10-year old, I remember telling my parents that I wanted to be a writer when I grew up. I remember writing short stories as a pre-teen, poetry and school newspaper articles in high school, and being passionately addicted to Shakespeare in college.

But God wanted to blend that with a helping of sales content, so He provided me that first job with Jewel Tea Company, where I got my first real taste of sales. Then, He gave me a wide variety of selling situations to provide me with a broad base of experiences, which He knew would serve me well in the profession He had in mind for me. He gave me intense success as well as dismal failure so that I would be able to relate to both. When I got too involved in the business, He used adversity to draw me closer to Him.

Following my career working for someone else, He put me into business for myself, using most of the gifts and knowledge that He had given to me. In that role, He opened some doors and closed others, leading me in the path that He wanted me to go.

Then, He led me to a turn in the path, and a focus on something additional to the sales authority practice. He planned it, arranged all the details, told me about it, and then did it.

At this point, I spend about half my time working with Christian Executives via Truth@Work and on various writing projects, and about half my time on the sales authority business – consulting with companies who want help with their sales efforts and speaking at conventions and national sales meetings.

I am, at the moment, where He wants me to be.

I think that God has worked the same way with me in regard to my evolving position towards the institutional church. For years I thought that I was the guy who was out-of-bounds, who just didn't get what everyone else seems to have gotten. I was the one who had these miserable experiences with the professional Christians when others were content. For decades I thought the problem was me.

Now, I see that God orchestrated those experiences and planted those thoughts in me, because He wanted to bring me to the position that I now hold and advocate: That the institutional church system is not the Church, it is a man-made substitute for it.

It has occurred to me that as I moved, little by little, away from the institutional church, I came closer to God.

The further I got away from the institutional church, the closer I got to God.

It has been as if the institutional church system was like a deep smog that engulfed me, preventing me from seeing the world, and God, more clearly. As I slowly struggled out from under the smog, prompted by this series of disappointments and disillusionments with the professional Christians, I began to see more and more of God. He began to draw closer to me. I had my first experience with received "rhema" – a personal message from God -- at the DeColores retreat – a non-denominational, 'laity-led' retreat a few years after I had stopped going to church. I had the first prophetic word directed to me at a house church conference. When I received Elizabeth's prophecy, it had been years since I had been involved in an institutional church.

I felt God's presence with me, on a day-to-day basis, as I wrote a companion book, "*Is the Institutional Church Really the Church?*" On several occasions, I received words to say, and thoughts to incorporate. I could not have imagined that kind of closeness to God if I had stayed in the midst of the fog, thinking that going to church on Sunday was the heart of Christianity.

Recently, I've been prompted to write The Good Book on Business which uncovers the place that Biblical businesses have in the Kingdom of God. If you want to be challenged to see your career and your business in a whole new light, read the book. Your views on business will never be the same.

Looking back on my career, I can clearly see how God was with me every step of the way.

Looking back on my career, I can clearly see how God was with me every step of the way.

Chapter Twenty-Five:

A big lesson learned: What it means to be a Christian sales person

What does it mean to be a Christian salesperson? How do we navigate the turbulent water that marks the intersection of two powerful currents – the need to do good work and make a living, comingling with the desires of the heart to know and obey God?

It means that we develop an ongoing, ever unfolding relationship with God that evidences itself and exercises itself in a large way through our work.

It means that we understand that we are a Christian first, and a sales person next. That we understand the parable of salt & light. In a lost world, God wants His people to bring His light into every nook and cranny of this globe. As salespeople, we are charged with holding the torch for His Kingdom in every interaction, every prospect, every customer, every transaction, every job, and every employer.

But we are not on our own. In every circumstance, God is there, although it rarely seems so at the time. God provides the circumstances He wants for us, He provides His word to direct us, and sends people into our lives to foster our development. He'll work with

175

the circumstances of our lives to move us closer to Him and to impact our world for Him.

I started out seeing my career as a salesperson being totally separate from my Christian faith. Today, I see my career as a sales person as a fertile ground for God to do His work of gradually transforming me, as well as a great opportunity to shed His light into the darkness around me. I am His, and He put me here for a reason. I will be eternally grateful for the opportunity and challenge of being a Christian sales person.

ABOUT THE AUTHOR...

Dave is a consultant and speaker who helps his clients grow their sales and develop their people. Specializing in business-to-business selling situations, Dave creates effective sales systems and helps salespeople take their performance up a level.

He's acquired his message through real-life experience. Dave has been the number one salesperson in the country for two different companies in two distinct industries.

As the general manager of a start-up company, Dave directed that company's growth from $10,000 in monthly sales to over $200,000 in just 38 months.

Dave annually presents over 75 seminars and training programs. He has spoken in 47 states and 11 countries, and has authored 13 books.

He holds a B.A. degree from the University of Toledo, and a Master's from Bowling Green State University.

He and his wife live in Grand Rapids, MI and Sarasota, FL where he is a father, a step-father, an adoptive father, a foster father, and a grandfather.

Dave is a member of the Author's Guild, the Christian Businessmen's Committee, and the American Society For Training and Development.

He can be reached at:
Dave Kahle Management, LLC

Grand Rapids, MI and Sarasota FL

PO Box 523, Comstock Park, MI 39432
(800) 331-1287
(616) 451-9377
info@davekahle.com
www.DaveKahle.com

Dave Kahle is available to:

• Speak at your conference or convention.

• Create customized sales training programs for your outside sales force, inside sales force, or sales managers.

• Consult with you on issues relating to sales productivity.

Dave Kahle is available to speak with your group or help your business grow. Visit The Biblical Business Course:

www.thebiblicalbusiness.com

and take a class to begin your growth. Visit:

www.thesalesresourcecenter.com

Dave Kahle Management, LLC

Grand Rapids, MI and Sarasota FL

PO Box 523, Comstock Park, MI 39432

(616) 451.9377 www.davekahle.com

35548566R00104

Made in the USA
San Bernardino, CA
12 May 2019